The Institution of Civil Engineers

LR/LEND/001

Guidance notes and flow charts for

The Professional Services Contract

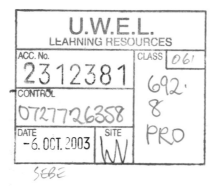
An NEC document

Thomas Telford

Published for the Institution of Civil Engineers by Thomas Telford Publishing, Thomas Telford Ltd, 1 Heron Quay, London E14 4JD.

The New Engineering Contract is a family of standard contracts, each of which has these characteristics:

- Its use stimulates good management of the relationship between the two parties to the contract and, hence, of the work included in the contract.

- It can be used in a wide variety of commercial situations, for a wide variety of types of work and in any location.

- It is a clear and simple document - using language and a structure which are straightforward and easily understood.

This Professional Services Contract is one of the NEC family

First edition 1994
Second edition June 1998

ISBN 0 7277 2635 8

British Library Cataloguing in Publication Data for this publication is available from the British Library.

Printed and bound in Great Britain by Thanet Press Limited, Margate, Kent

FOREWORD

The first edition of the Professional Services Contract (PSC) was published in 1994 as part of the New Engineering Contract (NEC) family of contracts. It was designed for the purpose of appointing professionals to carry out various roles in the NEC contracts (Project Manager, Supervisor, designers) and for the wider use of appointing professionals where the NEC was not used, or even when no construction work was required.

As Employers have begun to appreciate the benefits of the PSC and the NEC principles on which it has been drafted, they are using it in many different circumstances. Its structure permits wide flexibility in the choice of different options of payment to the Consultant, as well as in the allocation of risk between the Parties. Its incorporation of established management procedures has also been seen to be of considerable benefit.

With the increasing use of partnering arrangements, Employers have sought conditions of contract which are compatible with partnering. For the appointment of professionals, the PSC with its non-adversarial approach, has been seen to be well suited for this purpose. It is also anticipated that wider use of the PSC will be made by local authorities in appointing individuals and firms to provide professional services previously done in-house.

As a result of experience in using the PSC, and changes in the construction industry in the wake of the Latham Report published in 1994, it became evident that various amendments were required and that several improvements to the PSC could be made. Accordingly the second edition has been produced under the supervision of the NEC Panel together with these amended and augmented guidance notes. Flow charts, which have been used to check the drafting of clauses, have also been included. The Panel has also had the benefit of comments of the Construction Industry Council's Task Force which was established to investigate harmonisation of conditions of engagement (1994-5)

As in the first edition, the method of resolving disputes is adjudication. Since publication of the first edition, the UK Parliament has provided a right to adjudication for any disputing party in construction contracts (including professional services agreements) in the form of the UK Housing Grants, Construction and Regeneration Act 1996. Since the PSC, like all other standard forms of contract, does not comply with the Act, a secondary option Y(UK)2 has been included for use where the Act applies to UK contracts.

In this second edition the references of the secondary options have been changed to have the following prefixes:-

X	secondary options for general use
Y	secondary options for use only in a specific country, the initials (bracketed) of the country concerned following the prefix eg:- Y(UK)1, Y(UK)2.
Z	additional conditions of contract required by the *Employer* for a specific contract.

The second edition has been approved by the Council of the Institution of Civil Engineers for publication and use. Any comments and feedback from users should be sent to the Secretary of the NEC Panel at the Institution of Civil Engineers.

CONTENTS

ACKNOWLEDGEMENTS

The first edition of the NEC Professional Services Contract was drafted by Peter Higgins of the Institution of Civil Engineers with the assistance of Frank Griffiths of the Chartered Institute of Purchasing and Supply and Michael Coleman of the Association of Project Managers. Dr Martin Barnes then of Coopers & Lybrand advised on the co-ordination of the contract with the New Engineering Contract.

For the second edition of the NEC Professional Services Contract these Guidance Notes were produced by the Institution of Civil Engineers through its New Engineering Contract Panel and were mainly drafted by Bill Weddell and Tom Nicholson, with the assistance of Peter Higgins, as members of the New Engineering Contract Panel. The flowcharts were produced by John Perry, Ross Hayes and colleagues at the University of Birmingham.

The original New Engineering Contract was designed and drafted by Dr Martin Barnes then of Coopers and Lybrand with the assistance of Professor J. G. Perry of The University of Birmingham, T. W. Weddell then of Travers Morgan Management, T. H. Nicholson, Consultant to the Institution of Civil Engineers, A. Norman then of the University of Manchester Institute of Science and Technology and P. A. Baird, then Corporate Contracts Consultant, Eskom, South Africa.

The members of the New Engineering Contract Panel are:

P. Higgins, (Chairman) BSc, CEng, FICE, FCIArb.
P. A. Baird, BSc, CEng, FICE, M(SA)ICE, MAPM
Dr. M. Barnes, BSc(Eng), PhD, FEng, FICE, FCIOB, CIMgt, ACIArb,
       MBCS, FRSA, FInstCES, FAPM
L. T. Eames, BSc FRICS, FCIOB
T. H. Nicholson, BSc, CEng, FICE
M. A. Noakes, BSc, CEng, MICE, MIWEM
T. Pasley, MSc, CEng, FICE, FIHT.
Professor J. G. Perry, MEng, PhD, CEng, FICE, MAPM
N. C. Shaw, FCIPS, CEng, MIMechE
T. W. Weddell, BSc, CEng, DIC, FICE, FIStructE, ACIArb
F. N. Vernon, (Secretary), BSc, CEng, MICE

INTRODUCTION

The Professional Services Contract (PSC) has been developed as part of the New Engineering Contract (NEC) system of contract documents. The PSC has been drafted with the same objectives as the NEC and has adopted clauses from the Engineering and Construction Contract (ECC) where they were considered to be appropriate for the appointment of a professional organisation or person.

The purpose of the document is to form a standard contract for the appointment of consultants providing professional services to be used in engineering and construction generally. It can be used for the appointment of a project manager or a supervisor under an NEC contract and also for the appointment of persons fulfilling other roles associated with construction contracts (such as a designer responsible either directly to the Employer or to the Contractor in a construction contract) or for appointments of consultants in advance of construction (e.g. appointment of a project manager or designer during the early development stages of a project).

Its use however is not limited to projects where other NEC contracts are being used. It can be used where no construction works are to take place or where other forms of contract for construction are being used. When the PSC is used by a contractor (for instance, to appoint a designer as a subcontractor in a "design and construct" contract) the contractor has the role of "Employer" in the PSC. In such circumstances, the PSC can be used as a subcontract (ECC clause 26.3) with appropriate amendments. (See Appendices 3 and 4)

The contract has been drafted as a 'shell' contract which requires important information to be provided separately. The most critical document to be provided is the Scope. This contains the detailed requirements of the *Employer* and is frequently referred to within the PSC.

The purpose of these guidance notes is to explain the reasons for some of the provisions in the PSC and to provide guidance on how to use it. Where clauses are similar to those in the Engineering and Construction Contract, reference may be made to the ECC Guidance Notes for further explanation. The flow charts show the procedural logic on which the PSC is based and are published in this volume for reference.

The NEC conventions of using italics for terms which are identified in the Contract Data and capital initials for terms defined in the PSC have been used in these guidance notes. Neither the guidance notes nor the flow charts are contract documents, nor are they part of the Professional Services Contract. They should not be used for legal interpretation of the meaning of the PSC.

CONTRACT STRATEGY

The *Employer* chooses the contract strategy. This determines the specific professional *services* to be carried out, the basis of payment and the balance of risks between *Employer* and *Consultant*. The decision on contract strategy will identify the options from the Professional Services Contract to be chosen, the need for other provisions, and some of the material to appear in the Scope.

The main options

There are four types of payment mechanism available through the main options.

Option A	Priced contract with activity schedule
Option C	Target contract
Option E	Time based contract
Option G	Term contract

For a particular contract, one main option must be chosen. The clauses from the selected main option are combined with the core clauses and the clauses from the selected secondary options to provide a complete contract.

The main options provide different allocations of risk between the *Employer* and the *Consultant* and use different arrangements for payment to the *Consultant*:

- Option A is a lump sum priced contract in which the risks of being able to Provide the Services at the agreed prices in the *activity schedule* are largely borne by the *Consultant*.
- Option C is a target contract in which the financial risks are shared by the *Employer* and the *Consultant* in agreed proportions.
- Option E is a type of cost reimbursable contract in which the financial risk is largely borne by the *Employer*.
- Option G is a term contract in which various items of work are priced or stated to be on a time basis. Thus the risk of being able to perform the instructed Tasks at the agreed prices or *staff rates* is largely borne by the *Consultant*, whilst the *Employer* retains control over the individual Tasks to be carried out.

The ad valorem or percentage fee type of contract has not been included as an option. Under this arrangement, payments to the *Consultant* are an agreed percentage of the works construction cost. This implies that the cost of the *Consultant's* services is proportional to the cost of constructing the works. Its merits were carefully considered, but rejected for the following reasons:

- the *Consultant* has no incentive to produce an economical design or other service.
- the cost of construction is largely a function of the market and bears no relation to the cost of professional services
- the final cost of construction (and therefore the final fee) is not established until after construction is complete, whilst most professional costs are expended much earlier and even before construction starts.
- the effect of variations to the Scope on the payments due to the *Consultant* are difficult to assess.

Option A : Priced contract with activity schedule

Under this contract the *Consultant* is paid a lump sum for the *services*. An *activity schedule* is a list of the activities which the *Consultant* expects to carry out in Providing the Services. When it has been prepared and priced by the *Consultant*, the lump sum for each activity is the price to be paid by the *Employer* for that activity. The total of these prices is the *Consultant's* lump sum price for providing the whole of the *services*.

Option C : Target contract

Target contracts are sometimes used where the extent of work to be done is not fully defined or where anticipated risks are greater. Although used frequently in construction contracts, they have had limited application in consultancy contracts. The financial risk is shared between the *Consultant* and the *Employer* in the following way.

- The *Consultant* tenders a target price in the form of a priced *activity schedule*. The target price is the *Consultant's* estimate of Providing the Services and is defined as the total of the Prices
- The *Consultant* tenders his *staff rates*
- During the course of the contract the *Consultant* is paid the Time Charge which is the staff time for the *services* carried out priced at the appropriate *staff rates*. This is defined as the Price for Services Provided to Date
- At the end of the contract, if the final Price for Services Provided to Date is less than the final total of the Prices, the *Consultant* is paid his share of the difference according to the formula stated in the Contract Data. If the final Price for Services Provided to Date is greater than the final total of the Prices, the *Consultant* pays his share of the difference.

The Scope must be sufficiently descriptive to enable the *Consultant* to price the *services* in his tender.

The target price set at the Contract Date may change during the contract as the compensation events procedure is applied to changes in the Scope and other compensation events.

Option E : Time based contract

This is a cost reimbursable type of contract which should be used when the *services* cannot be defined sufficiently accurately for a lump sum to be quoted . In such circumstances the *Consultant* cannot be expected to take cost risks other than those which the control of his employees and other resources entails. He carries minimum risk and is paid the Time Charge (as defined by the *staff rates* stated in the contract).

Option G : Term contract

This contract provides for the appointment of a *Consultant* for a term (an agreed period of time). The *Consultant* prices a *task schedule* prepared in advance by the *Employer* as well as providing *staff rates* for different grades of staff. Each price on the *task schedule* is a lump sum for that particular item. Some items on the *task schedule* may be stated to be carried out on a time basis rather than for a lump sum price.

When the *Employer* requires specific services to be carried out by the *Consultant* he identifies a proposed Task by selecting individual items from the *task schedule*. Any items not on the *task schedule* are notified as compensation events and the compensation event assessment procedure is used to determine how each item is to be paid for. The *Consultant* carries out each Task only when he has been instructed to do so by the *Employer*.

The secondary options

After deciding the main option, the *Employer* may choose any of the secondary options which are:

Option X1	Price adjustment for inflation
Option X2	Changes in the law
Option X3	Multiple currencies (used only with Options A and G)
Option X4	Parent company guarantee
Option X5	Sectional Completion (not used with Option G)
Option X6	Bonus for early Completion (not used with Option G)
Option X7	Delay damages (not used with Option G)
Option X8	*Collateral warranty agreements*
Option X9	Transfer of rights
Option X10	*Employer's Agent*
Option X11	Termination by the *Employer*
Option Y(UK)1	The Construction (Design and Management) Regulations 1994
Option Y(UK)2	The Housing Grants, Construction and Regeneration Act 1996
Option Z	*Additional conditions of contract*

Any combination of secondary options may be used.

The Trust Fund secondary option included in the Engineering and Construction Contract has not been included in the PSC since the use of such an option in a contract for professional services is much less likely than in the case of a construction contract. If an *Employer* wishes to include such an option, the Trust Fund Option in the ECC should be used as a basis.

Option X1: Price adjustment for inflation

This option should be used if the *Employer* decides to accept the risk of inflation.

The price adjustment factor (PAF) is calculated on each anniversary of the Contract Date (cl X1.1) and is then used during the following year to make adjustments for inflation.

The *Employer* decides which published *index* to use, eg the Retail Price Index, and enters this in Part one of the Contract Data.

The *Consultant's staff rates* stated in Part two of the Contract Data may be either

- fixed, and thus not variable with changes in salary actually paid to individuals or
- variable with changes in salary paid to individuals

Fixed *staff rates*

In all the main options, an amount for price adjustment is calculated as stated in clauses X1.1 and X1.2 and for *expenses* adjustment in clause X1.6.

As the adjustment amounts are recorded separately in the amount due, in a target contract (Option C) the Price for Services Provided to Date continues to be comparable to the Prices (the target) for the purpose of calculating the *Consultant's* share.

Variable *staff rates*

Different clauses are used according to which main option applies, as follows:

Option A	Clauses X1.1	X1.2	X1.5	X1.6
Option C	Clauses X1.1	X1.3	X1.5	X1.6
Option E	Clause X1.6			
Option G	Clauses X1.1	X1.4	X1.5	X1.6

For a priced contract using an *activity schedule* (Option A), an amount for price adjustment is calculated as stated in clauses X1.1 and X1.2. The Time Charge to be used in the assessment of compensation events is adjusted to the Contract Date using clause X1.5 in order to maintain the time basis of the Prices.

For target contracts (Option C), an amount for price adjustment is added to the Prices (cl X1.3) so that the total of the Prices can be fairly compared with the final Price for Services Provided to Date (the Time Charge using variable *staff rates*) for calculating the *Consultant*'s share. The Time Charge to be used in the assessment of compensation events is adjusted to the Contract Date using clause X1.5.

For term contracts (Option G), a price adjustment is necessary only for the lump sum items in the *task schedule* using clause X1.4. The Time Charge to be used in the assessment of compensation events (including the lump sum items added to the *task schedule* under clause 55.1) is adjusted to the Contract Date using clause X1.5.

For all the main options (Options A, C, E and G), if the *expenses* are stated in the Contract Data as fixed prices and are not adjustable for inflation, an amount for *expenses* adjustment should be included in the amount due in accordance with clause X1.6.

Worked examples of the calculations of the amounts for price adjustment and *expenses* adjustment are given in Table 1.

Option X2 : Changes in the law   X2.1

This option reduces the effect on the *Consultant*'s costs and programme of the risk of changes to an *applicable law* which occurs after the Contract Date by making such a change a compensation event. Such changes can have a dramatic effect on the *Consultant*'s costs and his liability to make progress on the *services*.

The *Employer* should review the laws which could be relevant to the *services* and identify those where he is prepared to carry the risk of changes as *applicable law* in the Contract Data. These could be the *law of the contract* (cl 12.2), the law of the country where the services are to be provided, where the construction site is or where a major supplier is located.

For the purposes of this clause, the law includes a national or state statute, ordinance, decree, regulation (including building or safety regulations), by-law of a local or other duly constituted authority and other delegated legislation.

Table 1 - Option X1 - Price adjustment for inflation - Worked Examples

	Contract Date	1st Anniversary	2nd Anniversary
(i) Price Adjustment			
Index } (cl X1.1) PAF }	100 0.0	105 0.05	110 0.10
(a) Fixed *staff rates* (Options A, C, E and G) Change in PSPD Change in price adjustment amount (cl X1.2)	NO PRICE ADJUSTMENT	£20,000 £20,000 x 0.05 = £1,000	£20,000 £20,000 x 0.10 = £2,000
(b) Variable *staff rates*			
Option A and Option G (lump sum items only) Change in PSPD Change in price adjustment amount (Option A - cl X1.2. Option G - cl X1.4)	NO PRICE ADJUSTMENT	£20,000 £20,000 x 0.05 = £1,000	£20,000 £20,000 x 0.10 = £2,000
Staff rates for compensation event assessment (cl X1.5)	NO ADJUSTMENT	Current *staff rate* ÷ 1.05	Current *staff rate* ÷ 1.10
Option C Change in PSPD Addition to Prices (cl X1.3)	NO ADJUSTMENT	£20,000 £20,000 x 0.05 ÷ 1.05 = £952.38	£20,000 £20,000 x 0.10 ÷ 1.10 = £1818.18
Staff rates for compensation event assessment (cl X1.5)	NO ADJUSTMENT	Current *staff rate* ÷ 1.05	Current *staff rate* ÷ 1.10
(ii) Fixed *expenses* adjustment			
Options A, C, E and G Change in fixed *expenses* Change in *expenses* adjustment amount (cl X1.6)	NO EXPENSES ADJUSTMENT	£2,000 £2,000 x 0.05 = £100	£2,000 £2,000 x 0.10 = £200

Option X3 : Multiple currencies (used only with Options A & G)

X3.1   This option is used (in conjunction with main options A and G only) when it is intended that payment to the *Consultant* should be made in more than one currency and that the risk of changes in the exchange rates should be carried by the *Employer*.

The *Employer* should state in the Contract Data which items of work are to be paid for in currencies other than the *currency of this contract*, what those currencies are, the maximum amounts payable in each currency and the *exchange rates* to be used in calculating the payments. *Exchange rates* are usually those published some two weeks before the *Consultant* submits his offer to the *Employer*. Any subsequent movement of the *exchange rates* is therefore at the *Employer*'s risk. No provision is made for multiple currencies in main Options C and E because the *Consultant* is paid the Time Charge.

Option X4 : Parent company guarantee

X4.1   This option should be included where the *Employer* requires the greater security provided by the parent company for the performance of the *Consultant*.

Option X5: Sectional Completion (not used with Option G)

X5.1   This option should be included when the *Employer* requires parts of the *services* to be completed by key dates before the whole of the *services*. The parts are called *sections* each of which should be identified in the Contract Data part one, with a *completion date* for each. Completion of the *sections* is followed by Completion of the whole of the *services*. The *sections* do not make up the whole of the *services* but establish key dates. Delay damages and bonus for early completion can be related to *section completion dates* by using Options X7 and X6 respectively.

Option X6: Bonus for early Completion (not used with Option G)

X6.1   Where Completion as early as possible would benefit the *Employer*, whether of all or a *section* of the *services*, the *Employer* can use this option to achieve early Completion. The bonus calculated in accordance with this clause will be included in the assessment occurring at Completion of the whole (or *section*) of the *services*.

Option X7: Delay damages (not used with Option G)

X7.1   Delay damages are the liquidated damages paid by the *Consultant* when he fails to complete the *services* (or *sections* of the *services* if option X5 is also used) by the Completion Date. Under English law and some other legal systems, if it is not included, delay damages are "at large" and the remedy open to the *Employer* is to bring an action for damages for the *Consultant*'s breach of contract. In this event, evidence of the actual damage suffered by the *Employer* is required.

The amount of delay damages should not exceed a genuine pre-estimate of the damage which will be suffered as a result of the *Consultant*'s breach. They are described as delay damages because these are not the only liquidated damages in the PSC. Interest on late payments as provided for in clause 51.4 is a form of liquidated damages.

Appropriate entries for delay damages should be made in the Contract Data. They may represent cost to the *Employer* caused by delayed start to another contract, or simply interest on the capital invested in the *services* of which the *Employer* has been deprived of the benefit. Damages greater than a genuine pre-estimate constitute a penalty and are not generally enforceable under English law.

Since delay damages are amounts to be paid by the *Consultant*, appropriate deductions are made in the first assessment of the amount due, occurring after the Completion Date, and in subsequent assessments up to Completion.

X7.2 This clause protects the *Consultant* when he has paid delay damages and a later assessment of compensation events results in a delay to the Completion Date. This could arise when a compensation event occurs at a late stage or if an *Adjudicator* or *tribunal* changes the assessment of a compensation event, and the decision is made after delay damages have been paid.

Option X8: *Collateral warranty agreements*

X8.1 A *collateral warranty agreement* is an agreement entered into by the *Consultant* with purchasers or tenants or funding organisations (who are not the *Employer*) of an industrial or commercial development. It has the effect of binding the *Consultant* in contract, and creating legal liability toward parties other than the *Employer* which may not otherwise exist. Details of the *collateral warranty agreements* which the *Consultant* will be required to enter into should be stated in the Contract Data.

These details should include

- form of warranty agreement
- limitation period
- insurance requirements
- rights of assignment, including number of assignments to subsequent purchasers/tenants, permitted
- others providing warranty agreements

A requirement to enter into such agreements can represent a considerable extension of a *Consultant's* liability. Legal advice may be necessary and advisable. The British Property Federation has published model forms of collateral warranty which have been agreed by the ACE, RIAS, RIBA and RICS, after consultation with the Association of British Insurers.

Option X9 : Transfer of rights

X9.1
X9.2 The rights over drawings, documents, designs and the like prepared by the *Consultant* would normally remain with the *Consultant*. The core clauses recognise this but give the *Employer* entitlement to use any documents for the purposes stated in the Scope. If, in addition to this, the *Employer* wishes to obtain the rights for himself, this option should be chosen. The option permits the *Consultant* to use designs and documents for other work subject to restrictions and obligations set out by the *Employer* in the Scope.

Option X10 : *Employer's Agent*

X10.1 This option should be used where a corporate body wishes to appoint an individual, either from within its own organisation or an external consultant, to act as its agent under this contract. The *Agent* should be identified and the extent of the *Agent*'s authority defined in the Contract Data.

Option X11 : Termination by the *Employer*

X11.1 Under the core clauses the *Employer* is entitled to terminate following the substantial failure of the *Consultant* to carry out his obligations, on insolvency of the *Consultant*, or when the *Employer* no longer requires the *services*. This option gives a further power to the *Employer* to terminate the appointment of the *Consultant* for a reason not stated in the contract which might involve no default of the *Consultant*.

X11.2 This clause gives the *Consultant* entitlement to increased payment if the *Employer* terminates for a reason not stated in the contract. The 5% payment is arbitrary, but recognises that the *Consultant* has been deprived of some profit which he would have made if he had been permitted to continue with, and complete, the *services*.

Option Y(UK)1: The Construction (Design and Management) Regulations 1994

These regulations apply to the majority of construction work carried out in the United Kingdom. Hence this option should be used wherever the regulations apply to the *Consultant's* work. For each project a planning supervisor and a principal contractor are appointed with extensive powers to manage health safety and welfare at the design stage and throughout construction on site. Thus a *Consultant* doing design work or site supervision may be affected by the regulations.

The duties and powers of all parties involved in a project are set out in the regulations and are not repeated in the contract. This optional clause deals with payment arising from application of the regulations. The financial risk is shared between the *Employer* and the *Consultant*, the dividing line being based on what an experienced consultant could reasonably be expected to have foreseen.

Option Y(UK)2: The Housing Grants, Construction and Regeneration Act 1996

This option is prepared solely for use on contracts which are subject to the United Kingdom Housing Grants, Construction and Regeneration Act 1996 Part II ("the Act"). The option should not be used in other circumstances.

The two principles contained in this Act, which affect the NEC Professional Services Contract, are those related to payment and adjudication. The definition of a "construction contract" in this Act is wide ranging and can be found in Section 104. It covers not only an agreement to carry out "construction operations" but also "an agreement to do architectural, design or surveying work, or to provide advice on building, engineering, interior or exterior decoration or on the laying-out of landscape in relation to construction operations". Thus the Act will apply to many agreements made using the Professional Services Contract.

The definition of a "construction operation" can be found in Section 105(1) of the Act. The operations and contracts that are not subject to the Act are defined in Sections 105(2) and 106. In the United Kingdom (England, Wales, Scotland and Northern Ireland), the Parties to a contract should consider carefully whether the operation is subject to the Act before proceeding. If the operation or contract is subject to the Act, it is intended that, by incorporating Option Y(UK)2 into the contract, the provisions of the statutory Scheme for Construction Contracts do not become implied terms of the contract [S. 114(4)]. Parties must be aware that it is not possible to contract out of a statutory requirement.

Clause Y2.1 deals with the measurement of time periods in relation to the Act. Clauses Y2.2 to 2.4 and clause Y2.7 have been drafted with the intention of complying with Sections 109 to 113 and clauses Y2.5 and 2.6 have been drafted with the intention of complying with Section 108 of the Act.

Y2.1

In the NEC family of contracts periods of time are usually measured in weeks thus avoiding complications of rest days and statutory holidays in different countries in which these contracts are used. The Act, however, defines most periods as a number of days. S.116(3) of the Act states that Christmas Day, Good Friday and bank holidays are excluded from any period specified in the Act. Where the time period associated with the Act is referred to, that period has been stated in days in Option Y(UK)2.

The key periods affecting the procedure for payments when Option Y(UK)2 applies are illustrated in Figure 1 which includes references to the Act and to the Y(UK)2 clauses. Figure 1 should be referred to in conjunction with the following notes on clauses Y2.2 to Y2.4.

Y2.2, 2.3 and 2.7

These replacement and additional clauses in Y(UK)2 are drafted to accommodate Sections 109 to 111 of the Act. The *Employer* is now required to give notice to the *Consultant* of the payment to be made, and the basis on which the calculation is made. This is achieved by the replacement clause 51.1 in conjunction with the first bullet of additional clause 56.1.

It should be noted that core clauses 51.2 to 51.5 remain in place. In particular, clause 51.3 deals with disagreement with the assessment of an invoice whereas the Act [S 111(2)] deals with set-off or abatement which Y2.3 provides for in the additional clause 56.2.

The Act uses very specific language about what and when "payments become due", when particular notices are issued and defining the "final date for payment". The latter applies to each certified payment and not just to the final payment "after Completion of the whole of the *services*". Provision has been made for a different payment period to be stated in the Contract Data (reference replacement optional statement in Y2.7).

The additional clause 56.1 sets out time periods and circumstances to meet the requirements of S. 110 (1) and 110(2) of the Act. S. 110(1)(a) requires an "adequate mechanism for determining what payments become due under the contract and when". This mechanism is provided by the *Employer*'s certificate which is required to be issued by the date when payment becomes due (cl 51.1) which is 7 days after the assessment date (cl 56.1, 2nd bullet). S. 110(1)(b) requires that there should be "a final date for payment in relation to any sum which becomes due". This is 21 days, or the period stated in the Contract Data, after the date on which payment becomes due (cl 56.1 third bullet). The significance of the final date for payment is that if the *Employer* intends to withhold part of the amount due, he must give notice not later than a "prescribed period" ie 7 days before the final date for payment as indicated in S. 111 of the Act (cl 56.2).

Y2.4

Under S.112 of the Act, where a sum due is not paid by the final date for payment and no effective notice to withhold payment has been given, the *Consultant* has a right to suspend performance. This right can only be exercised if the *Consultant* gives 7 days' notice of his intention. The right to suspend ceases when payment is made in full. Under S. 112(4) of the Act, the Completion Date is, in effect, delayed by the period of suspension. The effect of the additional clause 60.4 is to treat such suspension as a compensation event. Thus, in addition to the extra time, the *Consultant* is entitled to additional costs resulting from the suspension.

Y2.5

The provisions in the Professional Services Contract for settling disputes do not comply with the Act although the principle of independent adjudication has been a key feature of the NEC family since its first publication in 1991. The purpose of Section 9 has always been to overcome where possible the causes of disputes and, in those cases where disputes may still arise, to facilitate their clear definition and early resolution. Hence this amendment replaces core clause 90 with new clauses which should comply with the Act. The intention of the new clauses is to retain the principles of the adjudication provisions in the PSC in managing disputes, and at the same time comply with the Act so that the fall-back "Scheme for Construction Contracts" does not apply.

Figure 2 should be referred to in conjunction with the notes on clauses Y2.5 and Y2.6.

The new clauses require a meeting to be held to discuss any matter of dissatisfaction, with a view to resolving the matter. If this procedure fails to resolve the matter, a dispute arises after which either Party can give notice of his intention to refer it to adjudication. The remaining procedure in the clause is similar to that in core clause 90.

Y2.6

Y(UK)2 clause 90 supersedes core clause 91.1 which is deleted. The new clause 91.1 extends the procedure for a meeting to resolve a matter of dissatisfaction, to include a subcontractor, where the relevant matter is one which involves the subcontractor. The new clause 91.3 requires the *Consultant* who is a subcontractor under the PSC to attend a meeting of the main contract parties, which is held to deal with a matter of dissatisfaction common to both contract and subcontract. Core clauses 91.2 and 91.3 are retained, but the latter has been renumbered 91.4.

Option Z: *Additional conditions of contract*

This option should be used where the *Employer* wishes to include additional conditions. These should be carefully drafted in the same style as the core and option clauses using the same defined terms and other terminology. They should be carefully checked for consistency with the other conditions.

Additional conditions should be used only when absolutely necessary to accommodate particular needs, such as those peculiar to the country in which the work is to be done. The flexibility of the PSC main and secondary options minimises the need for additional conditions. Additional conditions should not be used to limit how the *Consultant* is to do the work in the contract as this is part of the function of the Scope.

Construction Act - Payment Periods - May 1998
Professional Services Contract

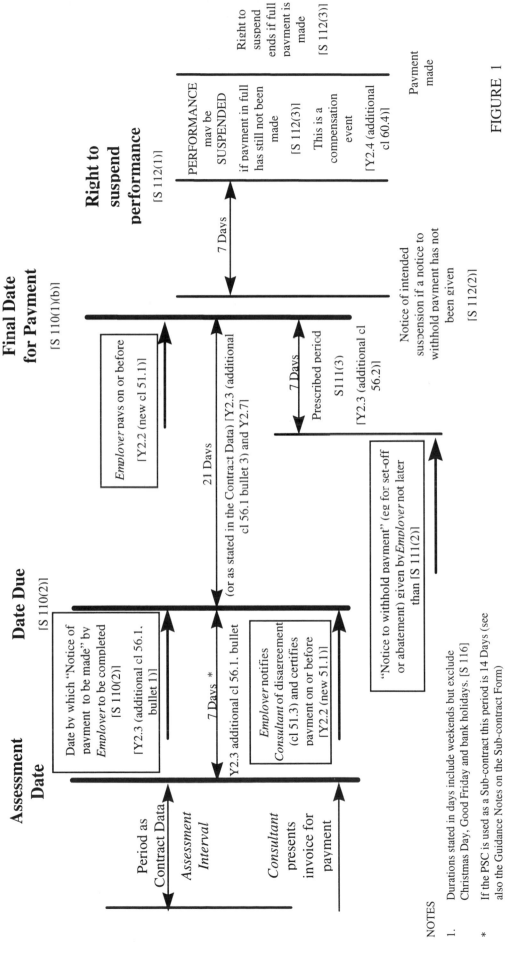

FIGURE 1

NEC Professional Services Contract

Amendments to Comply with Adjudication Provisions of the HGCR Act 1996

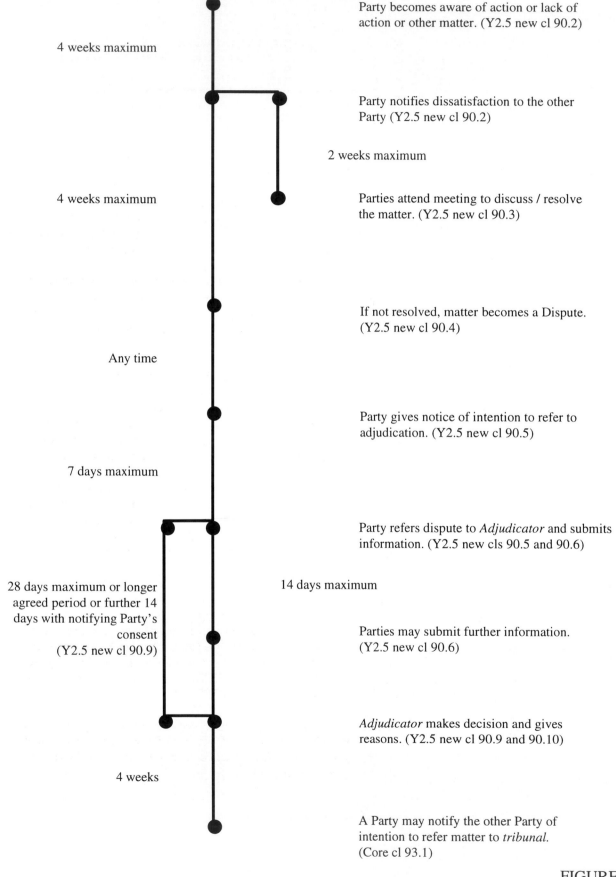

4 weeks maximum

Party becomes aware of action or lack of action or other matter. (Y2.5 new cl 90.2)

Party notifies dissatisfaction to the other Party (Y2.5 new cl 90.2)

2 weeks maximum

4 weeks maximum

Parties attend meeting to discuss / resolve the matter. (Y2.5 new cl 90.3)

If not resolved, matter becomes a Dispute. (Y2.5 new cl 90.4)

Any time

Party gives notice of intention to refer to adjudication. (Y2.5 new cl 90.5)

7 days maximum

Party refers dispute to *Adjudicator* and submits information. (Y2.5 new cls 90.5 and 90.6)

28 days maximum or longer agreed period or further 14 days with notifying Party's consent (Y2.5 new cl 90.9)

14 days maximum

Parties may submit further information. (Y2.5 new cl 90.6)

Adjudicator makes decision and gives reasons. (Y2.5 new cl 90.9 and 90.10)

4 weeks

A Party may notify the other Party of intention to refer matter to *tribunal*. (Core cl 93.1)

FIGURE 2

14

BASIS OF THE APPOINTMENT OF A CONSULTANT

The contract between the *Employer* and a *Consultant* will normally consist of the following:

- a letter or form of offer from the *Consultant*,
- the Contract Data part one (completed by or in conjunction with the *Employer*),
- the Contract Data part two completed by the *Consultant*,
- an *activity schedule* (Options A and C),
- a *task schedule* (Option G),
- the Scope
- a letter of acceptance from the *Employer* and
- form of agreement (if any)

Contract Data

The purpose of the Contract Data for a particular contract is to identify the terms printed in italics in the conditions of contract (cl 11.1) and to provide the information that some clauses state is in the Contract Data. The Contract Data thus completes the conditions for a particular contract.

Part one of the Contract Data is prepared by the *Employer* and identifies his requirements. The wording of the required statements is given in the PSC. This wording should be reproduced (but preferably not photocopied) with the various statements completed with the information relating to the particular contract.

Statements which must be included in all contracts are first listed followed by optional statements. The introductory explanatory sentences (printed in bold) should be omitted. Only those statements which are needed for the particular contract should be included. In order to avoid lengthy entries for certain items it may be convenient to list them in a separate document which can then be referenced in the Contract Data.

The completed part one of the document is normally issued to a consultant together with the prepared part two, which he is required to complete. It will identify other documents (e.g. *activity schedule, task schedule*) which are to be priced by the *Consultant* and submitted to the *Employer* with the completed part two of the Contract Data.

Further notes and a worked example of a completed Contract Data are given in Appendix 2.

Activity schedule
(Options A and C)

This document is a list of the activities which the *Consultant* will need to carry out in order to Provide the Services. It should be prepared and priced by the *Consultant* but the *Employer* can state his required framework for the document or a list of the minimum items to be included in his instructions to tenderers.

The price entered by the *Consultant* for each activity is a lump sum, not a unit rate. In Option A the *Consultant* is paid for activities completed at each assessment date. In Option C, the total of the Prices in the *activity schedule* is the target price.

***Task schedule* (Option G)**

The *task schedule* is prepared by the *Employer* and describes (in sufficient detail to enable the *Consultant* to price them) individual items which the *Employer* is likely to require the *Consultant* to carry out. Other items may be included in the *task schedule* to be paid for on a time basis using the Time Charge.

The *Consultant* prices each item in the *task schedule* which is not time based and quotes *staff rates* in part two of the Contract Data for use in calculating the Time Charge. When the *Employer* identifies a proposed Task he wishes to have carried out, he selects the required items from the *task schedule,* notifies any which are not on the *task schedule* as a compensation event and instructs the *Consultant* to submit his estimate for the Task. The *Consultant* does not carry out a Task until instructed to do so.

Scope

The conditions of contract refer to matters which must be covered by the Scope. These matters are summarised in Table 2.

In addition to the requirements made necessary by the particular contract, the Scope should contain further information describing what the *Consultant* is to provide. The extent of the Scope will vary between appointments. It will vary according to how well defined the *Employer*'s requirements are, what the particular *Consultant*'s tasks are and what function the *Consultant* is to perform.

Many professional bodies and organisations have prepared schedules of tasks as have many employers' organisations. If assistance is needed in preparing the Scope, it will normally be appropriate to appoint a consultant for that purpose or to prepare it jointly with the selected *Consultant.*

Form of Agreement

The creation of a contract can be by means of acceptance of a tender or a revised tender or by means of acceptance by the *Consultant* of a counter-offer prepared by or on behalf of the *Employer.* A binding contract is thus created, although some *Employers* may require such acceptance being subject to a formal agreement. A suitable form of agreement is included in Appendix 1 but *Employers* often have their own standard forms. Essentially they record the agreement between the two Parties.

Table 2

REFERENCES TO THE SCOPE IN THE CONTRACT

> This table does not include other uses of the Scope not specifically required by the clauses e.g. any specific levels of skill and care required (GN on cl 21.2).

Clause	Item	Comment
11.2(5) Identified and defined terms	Specifies and describes the *services*. States any constraints.	General definition of Scope.
11.2(8)	Definition of Completion	Reference to Scope
11.2(10)	Definition of Defect	Reference to Scope
13.5 Communications	Form of documents for retention.	Form of retained copies stated in Scope eg. microfilm, originals.
18.1 Illegal and impossible requirements	*Consultant* to notify	*Employer* to instruct changes to the Scope.
20.2 The *Employer*'s obligations	*Employer* may change the Scope	Only the *Employer* can change the Scope.
21.1 The *Consultant*'s obligations	Provides the services	In accordance with the Scope.
23.1 Co-operation	Information exchange with Others.	List of information the *Consultant* is to obtain from Others and list of information to be provided by the *Consultant* to Others.
31.2 The programme	Inclusions in programme.	Dates constraining the work. List of activities to be carried out by the *Employer* and Others. Any specific information which the *Consultant* is to show on the programme, e.g. key dates, approvals..
40.1 Quality management system	System requirements.	The Scope should describe what quality management system the *Consultant* will be required to operate.
40.2 Quality management system	Information in quality plan.	The Scope should identify any specific information to be shown in the quality plan and quality policy statement.
50.2 Assessing the amount due	Details to be provided with the *Consultant*'s invoices.	The *Employer* should set out any information he will require from the *Consultant* with each invoice to enable him to check the invoice for correctness.
60.1(1) (4) & (7) Compensation events	*Employer* changes Scope. Others do not work as stated in Scope *Employer* withholds acceptance.	Compensation events related to Scope
63.6 Assessing compensation events	Proposed staff rates for change to Scope.	*Consultant* to propose staff rates for people for whom there are no *staff rates*.
70.1 The Parties' use of material	Use of material by the *Employer*.	The *Employer* must state the purposes for which he will be using any material provided by the *Consultant* (e.g. construction, maintenance, extension, rebuilding).
Option X4 X4.1 Parent company guarantee	Form of guarantee.	If a guarantee is required, the *Employer* is to provide a proforma guarantee.
Option X9 X9.1 Transfer of rights	Rights over material	Requirements stated in Scope.
Option X9 X9.2 Transfer of rights	*Consultant*'s use of material	The Scope should state any restrictions and obligations on the *Consultant*'s use of material provided by him.

EXPLANATORY NOTES

1. General

CORE CLAUSES

Actions 10

10.1 This clause states the general obligations of the Parties to act "as stated in this contract". The same obligation of the Adjudicator links with his obligation in the NEC Adjudicator's Contract. The specific duties of the *Employer* the *Consultant* and the *Adjudicator* and the procedures to be followed are stated elsewhere in the contract and are in the present tense, i.e. as at the time of the action, rather than in the form `The *Consultant* shall . . .'. Where actions are permitted but not obligatory, the term `may' is used.

The inclusion of the requirement for the Parties to act in a spirit of mutual trust and co-operation is based on a recommendation in the Latham Report ("Constructing the Team"). This report, published in July 1994, was the final report of an investigation by Sir Michael Latham into procurement and contractual arrangements in the UK construction industry.

The obligation of the *Adjudicator* to act "in a spirit of independence" links with clause 92.1 and with his obligation to be impartial in the NEC Adjudicator's Contract.

**Identified and defined 11
terms** 11.1 The main definitions used in the contract are listed in clause 11.2. Other definitions appear in optional clauses where they are specific to a particular option. Capital initial letters are used in the PSC for defined terms to distinguish them from undefined terms. The same convention of italics and capital initials is used in these guidance notes as in the PSC itself.

11.2(2) The defined term "Others" provides a convenient means of reference (by stating the exceptions) to people and organisations not directly involved in the contract.

11.2(3) Contracts come into existence by various means - sometimes by means of a counter-offer and its acceptance, sometimes after extended negotiations and discussions. The Contract Date is used to define the date when the contract comes into existence, regardless of the means by which this is achieved.

It is very important to establish and document the means by which the contract came into existence. If this is not done, there is a significant risk of later difficulties if a dispute about the contract arises.

11.2 (4), These sub-clauses define the two key terms used in clause 21.1 to state
(5) what the *Consultant* is to do under the contract.

Within both definitions, a broad title of the *services* would be identified in the Contract Data, eg. "project management of the construction of a new factory at Swindon".

The *Employer* should use the Scope to specify and describe the *services* as comprehensively as possible including what he is expecting to achieve as a result of the contract and a statement of any constraints which the *Consultant* is to abide by.

The clauses of the PSC contain many references to information and requirements which should be specified in the Scope. These are summarised in Table 2. The *Employer* can change the Scope during the course of the contract (cl 20.2).

11.2(7)   The *completion date* stated in the Contract Data may be changed as a consequence of a compensation event.

11.2(8)   The Scope must state what work is to be done before Completion can be certified under clause 30.2. This, together with the second bullet, avoids the uncertainty associated with terms such as "substantial completion".

11.2(9)   The definition of the Accepted Programme allows for the two situations where there may or may not have been a requirement for the *Consultant* to submit a programme with his tender. A tender programme is identified in the Contract Data and becomes the Accepted Programme when the contract comes into existence.

11.2(10)   A Defect is simply something which the *Employer* realises will not satisfy his requirements as stated in the Scope. This may be because the *Consultant* has not provided the *services* properly or it may be that the initial Scope did not accurately reflect the *Employer*'s intentions and therefore has to be changed under clause 20.2, triggering a compensation event under clause 60.1(1). Clause 41 (Correcting Defects) deals further with the consequences of a Defect.

11.2(11)   The Time Charge is defined in relation to *staff rates* and staff time expended on the *services*. For many commissions the entries for *staff rates* in part two of the Contract Data will have fixed hourly, weekly or monthly rates entered against them. On other occasions, the *staff rates* will need to be defined in relation to salary.

The Time Charge is used in the PSC in two ways:

- for assessment of compensation events for all options and
- for evaluation of the amount due to the *Consultant* for the *services* in Option E (time based contract), Option C (target contract) and partially in Option G (term contract).

The *staff rates* are effectively the price charged for staff on a time basis. They will include for all costs to the *Consultant* including basic salary, any additional payments or benefits and social costs such as insurances or pension payments. Office expenses, including rental and heating, non-recoverable staff time and administrative staff who are not chargeable, together with the *Consultant*'s general overheads and profit should also be allowed for in the *staff rates*.

The *staff rates* can conveniently be established in one of three ways:

- rates for named staff,
- rates for categories of staff or
- rates related to salaries paid to staff.

The choice between these alternatives will depend on the type of *services* to be carried out. Where the *services* are to be provided by one person or a few staff identified in advance, individual rates for those staff would be most appropriate. If it becomes necessary to change staff, a new rate is readily negotiated based on different salary and other matters. Rate adjustments for inflation, if necessary, can be based either on actual salary adjustments or by using Option X1, Price adjustment for inflation.

If the *services* are to be carried out by a larger number of staff, but having clearly defined duties or responsibilities, the second method of defining *staff rates* is appropriate. The services of the supervisor on a large site is an example. The various posts can readily be categorised, and hourly, daily or weekly rates given for staff in that category. If price adjustment for inflation is needed, Option X1 is used.

If neither of these methods is suitable, *staff rates* should be linked to salary. This method has wide application and does not artificially reduce or increase the payments made. The difficulties of categorisation are avoided, but care needs to be taken to define which staff time is recoverable and which is not. The *staff rates* would then be stated as a multiplier on salary.

In this third method, the *Employer* has least control over costs. Under Options C, E and G, provision is made for forecasts at specified intervals by the *Consultant*, with explanations of changes since the last forecast (cl 21.4).

Many *Employers* have their own model for defining salaries and multipliers for staff and for identifying who may allocate time and who is included in the multiplier.

Communications

13

13.1   The phrase `in a form which can be read, copied and recorded' includes a letter sent by post, telex, cable, electronic mail, facsimile transmission, and on disc, magnetic tape or similar electronic means.

13.3   A reply has to be made within the *period for reply*. Where a variety of different communications is to be handled, e.g. requests for information, acceptance of contractors' designs, general correspondence, different *periods for reply* may be necessary. If so, they can be separately listed in the Contract Data. There is no need for the PSC to provide for extending the *period for reply* as the Parties can do this by mutual agreement.

13.4
(13.7)   The PSC contains a number of situations in which the *Employer* must either accept or reject a document which contains proposals submitted by the *Consultant*. The *Consultant* carries the risk of the *Employer* withholding acceptance because the proposal does not comply with the Scope or for a reason stated in the contract. Withholding acceptance for any other reason is a compensation event (cl 60.1(7)). This arrangement gives the *Employer* freedom to withhold acceptance for any reason but limits the *Consultant's* risk associated with this freedom. The Employer should ensure that the Scope states his requirements clearly, especially in areas which could directly affect his interests, eg. his procurement strategy for further contracts for design, supply, construction etc.

13.5   The *Employer* must decide the period during which the *Consultant* must keep the various documents he has used in doing his work. This period is entered in part one of the Contract Data.

13.6   The requirement to separate notifications from other communications is included to avoid important matters being missed.

Early warning   **15**

15.1   The intention of this clause is to oblige each Party to warn the other of anything which could affect the outcome of the contract as expressed in the three bullets and then to promote co-operation between the Parties to mitigate any adverse effects.

An early warning may often be associated with the notification of a future compensation event and in some cases one notification may cover both. For instance, the *Consultant* may give early warning of a probable change in the law (Option X2) and notify a compensation event at the same time. However, if the change is only a possibility, an early warning on its own may be appropriate and the notification of a compensation event deferred.

In contrast, the *Employer* may instruct a change in the Scope and notify it as a compensation event under clause 60.1(1). Both Parties are then aware of the instruction, assessments will be provided under the compensation event procedure and no early warning should be necessary.

Clauses 61.4 and 63.3 provide a sanction for failure by the *Consultant* to give early warning of a matter when he became aware of it, by reducing the payment due to him from any related compensation events.

It is probable that the *Employer* will require additional reporting by the *Consultant* - for example on any changes to potential construction costs. Such additional requirements should be stated in the Scope.

15.2
15.3   These clauses provide a procedure for the Parties to meet following an early warning and to cooperate in finding solutions and deciding actions.

Ambiguities and inconsistencies   **16**

16.1   This clause is intended to ensure that action is taken as soon as possible to deal with ambiguities and inconsistencies which are noticed in the contract documents. There is no stated precedence of documents and the *Employer* has the responsibility of instructing resolution of the problem. An instruction which results in a change to the Scope or a change to a previous decision would be a compensation event (clause 60.1 (1) or (5)) as would an instruction covered by clause 60.1(9). Also, in Option G, an instruction which corrects a mistake in the *task schedule* is a compensation event under clause 60.3.

Health and safety   **17**

17.1   In many countries there are laws which place considerable responsibilities upon employers, employees and others in relation to health and safety. Generally, the sanctions for non-compliance are criminal in nature as opposed to civil. It is not appropriate or necessary to reproduce or summarise this legislation in contract documents. The various parties to the PSC each have their obligations under statute and the general law. It is necessary, however, to include in the contract any particular requirements which the *Employer* has. These requirements are referred to in the Contract Data and stated in detail in the Scope. They may include such matters as:

- the *Employer*'s own internal safety procedures and
- identifying who carries out specific roles required by statute.

If the services are to be provided in the UK and the CDM Regulations 1994 apply, Option Y(UK)1 should be included in the contract.

Illegal and impossible requirements   **18**

18.1   A change to the Scope in order to resolve a matter which requires the *Consultant* to do anything which is illegal or impossible is a compensation event (cl 60.1(1)).

MAIN OPTION CLAUSES

Option G: Term contract

Identified and defined terms	**11** 11.2(18)	Work is carried out by the *Consultant* only after the *Employer* has instructed a Task under clause 55.5.

The other main option clauses in Section 1 are definitions concerning payment. Guidance on these is included in Section 5.

2. The Parties' main responsibilities

This section sets out the *Employer*'s and the *Consultant*'s main responsibilities. Other sections deal with particular responsibilities appropriate to the section heading.

CORE CLAUSES

The *Employer*'s obligations	**20** 20.1	This clause relates to the compensation events stated in clauses 60.1(2) and (3).
	20.2	The authority to change the Scope belongs exclusively to the *Employer*. Neither the *Consultant* nor the *Adjudicator* can change the Scope.
	20.3	This clause recognises the professional nature of the *services* being provided. If the *Employer*'s instructions cannot be complied with, the *Consultant* should advise the *Employer* of the fact and suggest alternative measures to achieve the *Employer*'s requirements.
The *Consultant*'s obligations	**21** 21.1	This clause states the *Consultant*'s basic obligation.
	21.2	This clause states the level of skill and care required of the *Consultant*. If the *Employer* requires any specific level of care or performance in providing parts of the *services* this should be stated in the Scope.
People	**22** 22.1	The *key persons* named in the Contract Data should be the persons named by the *Consultant* and accepted by the *Employer* to do the jobs most critical to Providing the Services. The *Consultant* does not have the right to replace a *key person* at will but can only replace him if the replacement is acceptable to the *Employer*. If the *Employer*'s reason for not accepting a proposed replacement for a *key person* is not the reason stated in this clause, a compensation event occurs (cl 60.1(7)).
Co-operation	**23**	The duty of the *Consultant* to co-operate with Others has been expressed in the PSC in general terms only.
	23.1 23.2	On large projects there may be several consultants and other organisations. Details of these and the services they are required to provide should be stated in the Scope. On some projects the lead consultant who is responsible for co-ordinating the work of all other consultants should also be identified in the Scope.

It is important that planning and programming of the work of the various consultants and Others are carried out before the start of the contract. The *Consultant* is not responsible for the failure of other parties to carry out their work in accordance with the Accepted Programme unless the failure is caused by the *Consultant* not co-operating. The exchange of information on health and safety matters is particularly important in order to comply with the law as well as with the contract.

Subconsulting   **24**

24.1 to
24.3   These clauses permit the *Consultant* to arrange for parts of the *services* to be provided by Subconsultants, provided the *Employer* accepts the proposed Subconsultant and the subcontract conditions to be used. Acceptance of the Subconsultant cannot be withdrawn later, providing his appointment complies with these clauses, but the *Consultant* is responsible for the Subconsultant's performance under clause 24.1.

The PSC may be used by a *Consultant* to appoint a Subconsultant if it is adapted as explained in Appendix 4.

Approval from Others   **25**

25.1   The *Employer* should state in the Scope what approvals he has obtained. Under this clause the *Consultant* is required to obtain any other approvals which are necessary. If the *Consultant* is required to report on the status of the approvals he is required to obtain, this should also be stated in the Scope. If for some reason, obtaining approvals is delayed, the *Consultant* (or *Employer*) should give early warning under clause 15.1 and the Accepted programme may need to be changed. If approvals cannot be obtained, eg. planning permission is refused, the *Consultant* should notify the *Employer* of an illegality or impossibility under clause 18.1, after which action lies with the *Employer*.

Access   **26**

26.1   Where the *Consultant* needs access to a person, place or thing in order to Provide the Services, the *Employer* is required to provide it by an access date in accordance with the contract.

Provision is made in Part one of the Contract Data for the *Employer* to list the accesses which the *Consultant* will need and state the *access date* which has been arranged for each.

Provision is also made in Part two of the Contract Data for the *Consultant* to state any additional accesses he will require together with the relevant *access dates.*

During the course of the contract, access dates later than those stated in the Contract Data may be agreed by the Parties and included in the Accepted Programme. A compensation event is triggered under clause 60.1(2) if an access is provided late.

MAIN OPTION CLAUSES

Option A: Priced contract with activity schedule

The *Consultant*'s   **21**
obligations   21.4   Forecasts of the total *expenses* are required for budget purposes, updated at regular intervals. They enable the *Employer* to judge the likely final cost to him of *expenses* which are additional to the Prices.

Option C: Target contract

The *Consultant*'s obligations	**21**
	21.5

Forecasts of the total Time Charge and *expenses* are required for budget purposes. They enable the *Employer* to judge the likely final Price for Services Provided to Date, the likely *Consultant*'s share and the likely cost to him of *expenses*. Forecasts are updated at regular intervals.

Option E: Time based contract

The *Consultant*'s obligations	**21**
	21.5

Forecasts of the total Time Charge and *expenses* are required for budget purposes. They enable the *Employer* to judge the likely final cost to him of the *services*. Forecasts are updated at regular intervals.

Option G: Term contract

The *Consultant*'s obligations	**21**
	21.5

Forecasts of the total Time Charge and *expenses* are required for budget purposes. They enable the *Employer* to judge the likely final cost to him of the time based items and the *expenses* for the Tasks instructed before the date of the forecast. The lump sum prices for the other items in the Tasks are additional to the forecasts.

3. Time

CORE CLAUSES

Completion   30

         30.1   The Completion Date (defined in cl 11.2(7)) may be of minor importance in some professional services contracts but, in others, it can be critical in co-ordinating the work of several consultants.
Provision is made in the Contract Data for the *completion date*

- to be specified by the *Employer* in Part one or
- to be tendered by the *Consultant* in Part two.

The Completion Date may be changed from the *completion date* as a result of a compensation event.

It is essential that a *completion date* is stated in the contract in either Part one or Part two of the Contract Data. If this is not done, the time effects of compensation events cannot be applied.

         30.2   The *Employer* is responsible for certifying Completion, as defined in clause 11.2(8), within one week of it being achieved.

The programme   31

         31.1   Provision is made for a programme either agreed at the Contract Date or to be prepared by the *Consultant* and submitted at an early stage in the contract. In the latter event the *Employer* is required to respond within two weeks (cl 31.3) but if the reply is non-acceptance, the *Consultant* is required to re-submit within the *period for reply*.

The Accepted Programme as defined in clause 11.2(9) is an important document for administering the contract. It enables the *Employer* and the *Consultant* to monitor progress and to assess the effects of compensation events. It identifies when particular actions are needed from the Parties.

31.2	This clause lists the information which the *Consultant* is required to show on each programme submitted for acceptance. Further information to be shown on the programme for a specific contract should be stated in the Scope (see. Table 2).

The *starting date* is the date when the *Consultant* can start work on the *services* and is used in clause 50.1 to fix the payment assessment dates throughout the contract.

31.3   This clause gives the reason why an *Employer* may decide not to accept a programme. Any failure by the *Employer* to accept a programme for reasons other than that stated in this clause, is a compensation event unless the programme does not comply with the Scope (cl 60.1(7)).

Revising the **32**
programme 32.1   This clause lists the matters which are to be shown on a revised programme. It should record the actual progress achieved on each operation and the re-programming of future operations. It should also show the effects of implemented compensation events and early warning matters. If a compensation event affects the timing of future operations, a revised programme indicating the effects is to be submitted as part of the *Consultant*'s quotation (cl 62.2). The revised programme should also show proposals for dealing with delays, Defects and any changes proposed by the *Consultant*.

32.2   No provision is made for the programme to be revised at stated intervals but either Party may initiate a revision under this clause.

MAIN OPTION CLAUSES

Option A: Priced contract with activity schedule

The programme **31**
31.4   This clause enables the timing of payments to be related to the programme.

Option C: Target Contract

The programme **31**
31.4   This clause relates the make-up of the Prices (the target) to the programme.

Option G: Term contract

The programme **31**
31.5   This clause enables the timing of payments within each Task to be related to the programme.

4. Quality

CORE CLAUSES

Quality management **40**
system 40.1 to   These clauses provide for the *Consultant* to operate a quality
40.3   management system to the extent required by the Scope. The *Employer* decides the extent of the quality management system. On one extreme he may require no quality management system at all.

On the other extreme he may require the operation of a fully certified quality assurance system under ISO standards. The quality management system required of the *Consultant* should recognise the equivalent requirements on other consultants or contractors and be compatible with them.

If the *Consultant* fails to provide the quality statement and quality plan as required by the Scope (cl 40.2), the *Employer* may, as a last resort, terminate the *Consultant's* appointment in accordance with clause 94.3.

Correcting Defects **41**

41.1   The period between Completion and the *defects date* is stated in the Contract Data. The length of the period will depend on the type of services being provided but will normally be between 6 months and a year. This clause requires the *Employer* to notify Defects until the *defects date*. The *Consultant* is required to notify uncorrected Defects at Completion (cl 11.2(8)) and any new Defects he becomes aware of after Completion and until the *defects date* which is the cut-off date for the *Consultant*'s responsibility to correct.

41.2   This clause requires the *Consultant* to correct all Defects, ie. so that the *services* are in accordance with the Scope (cl 11.2(10)). It does not require any admission by the *Consultant* of responsibility for the Defect but enables the *services* to be corrected with appropriate urgency to minimise disruption to the *Employer*'s project (See Figure 3).

41.3   This clause states the action that the *Employer* may take if the *Consultant* fails to correct a Defect in accordance with the contract (eg cl 41.2).

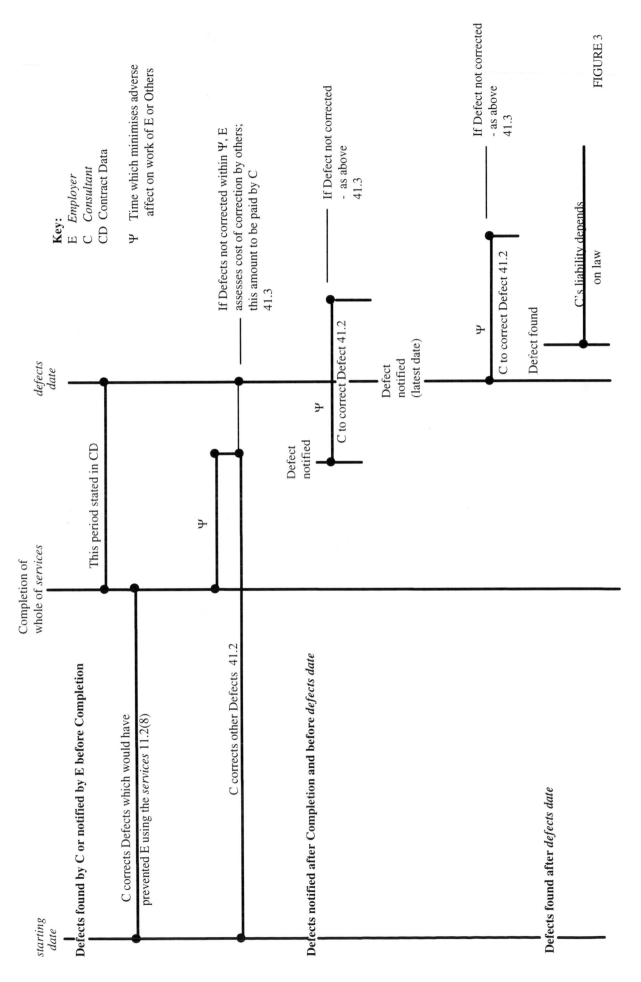

FIGURE 3

27

5. Payment

The payment mechanisms for the four main options are distinguished mainly by the use of two key terms:

- The Prices and
- The Price for Services Provided to Date.

Each term is defined in clause 11.2 for each main option.

The Prices

Option A (11.2(12))	The lump sum prices for each of the activities in the *activity schedule*.
Option C (11.2(12))	As Option A.
Option E (11.2(13))	The Time Charge.
Option G (11.2(14))	The Time Charge for items described as time based on the *task schedule* and the lump sum price in the *task schedule* for each other item.

The Price for Services Provided to Date

Option A (11.2(15))	The *Consultant* is paid the lump sum prices for activities from the *activity schedule* which have been completed at the assessment date. It is important that the *Consultant*, when compiling the *activity schedule*, defines activities, completion of which can be clearly recognised.
Option C (11.2(16))	Payment to the *Consultant* is as Option E. The Prices are the target and are compared with the Time Charge at the time of final payment to determine the *Consultant*'s share (cl 54)
Option E (11.2(16))	The *Consultant* is paid the Time Charge for services carried out.
Option G (11.2(17))	The *Consultant* is paid, for each Task, the Time Charge for time-based work completed and a proportion of the lump sums representing the proportion of work completed.

The following notes on Section 5 apply to the general and international use of the Professional Services Contract. The key periods affecting the procedure for payments are illustrated in Figure 4 which should be referred to in conjunction with the notes.

On contracts in the United Kingdom to which the Housing Grants, Construction and Regeneration Act 1996 Part II applies, Option Y(UK)2 should be incorporated. Reference should then be made to the separate notes on Option Y(UK)2 which include references to the necessary modifications and additions to core clauses.

Payment Periods
Professional Services Contract

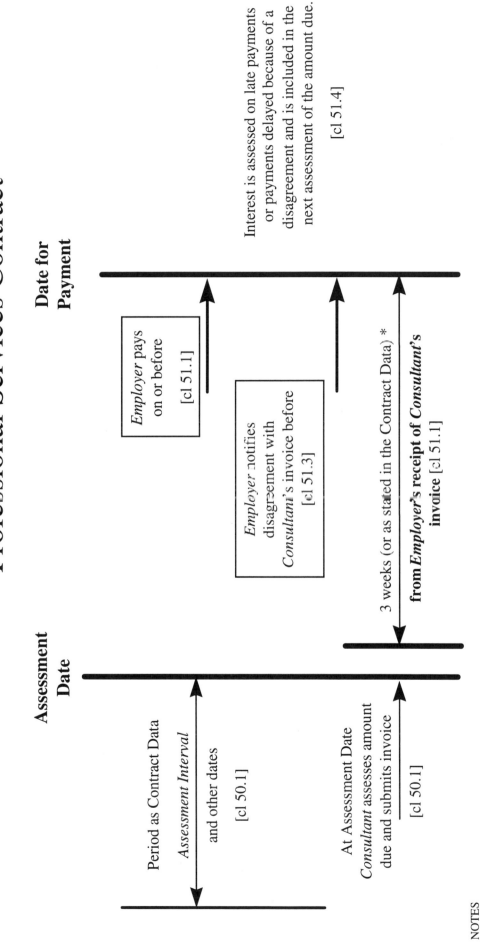

Assessment Date

Date for Payment

Period as Contract Data
Assessment Interval and other dates
[cl 50.1]

At Assessment Date
Consultant assesses amount due and submits invoice
[cl 50.1]

Employer notifies disagreement with *Consultant's* invoice before
[cl 51.3]

Employer pays on or before
[cl 51.1]

Interest is assessed on late payments or payments delayed because of a disagreement and is included in the next assessment of the amount due.
[cl 51.4]

3 weeks (or as stated in the Contract Data) *
from *Employer's* receipt of *Consultant's* invoice [cl 51.1]

NOTES

*   If the PSC is used as a Sub-contract this period is "4 weeks (or as stated in the Subcontract Data)" (see also the Guidance Notes on the Sub-contract Form)

FIGURE 4

29

CORE CLAUSES

Assessing the amount   **50**
        due   50.1   This clause determines the assessment dates. The subsequent dates when payment is due are calculated from the date when the *Employer* receives the *Consultant*'s invoice (cl 51.1). The first assessment date is decided by the *Consultant*, preferably after discussion with the *Employer*, to suit the internal procedures of both Parties. The Employer states the *assessment interval* in the Contract Data. The fourth main bullet determines the final assessment date which allows time for the correction of any Defects notified just before the *defects date* and subsequently for the assessment of the payment due from the *Consultant* of any uncorrected Defects which remain uncorrected (cl 41.3).

        50.2   The *Consultant* is required to make an assessment of the amount due at each assessment date. He is required to submit an invoice for the change in the amount due since the previous invoice and provide the details stated in the Scope to show how the amount due has been calculated.

        50.3   The main part of the amount due is the Price for Services Provided to Date as defined for each main option in clause 11.2.

Expenses

The amount due also includes the *expenses* incurred by the *Consultant* in Providing the Services. The items of *expenses* are defined in part one and part two of the Contract Data. The *Employer* should complete part one for any *expenses* for which he wishes to state the amount to be paid. The *Consultant* should complete part two for any additional *expenses* and the amount of payment he requires. Any expenses not so defined are not reimbursed to the *Consultant*, who must therefore make due allowance for them in pricing his offer , i.e. in the lump sums, *staff rates*, etc. as the case may be. Only *expenses* stated in the Contract Data are payable in addition to the Price for Services Provided to Date in all payment options.

Items of *expenses* which may be included in the Contract Data are photocopies, telephone, facsimile and package costs, postage, travel and hotel costs. Details of travel costs by public transport or private car should also be included as required.

Expenses should also include disbursements which are fees and charges paid by the *Consultant* on behalf of the *Employer*. Any such items which the *Employer* requires the *Consultant* to arrange for and pay e.g. fees for planning applications, advertising for site staff, should be listed as *expenses* in the Contract Data.

Pricing of *expenses* may be expressed in various forms. These include

- at net cost
- at cost plus..........percent
- lump sums and rates
- percentage of the Prices.

Payment **51**

51.1 Set-off is not specifically mentioned in this clause. Thus if the *Employer* has a legitimate claim against the *Consultant* the normal law of set-off will apply.

51.3 Where the *Employer* is not in agreement with an invoice submitted by the *Consultant*, he has to:

- pay the amount he does not dispute and
- explain to the *Consultant* why and where he disagrees.

The *Consultant* then has to correct the invoice to the *Employer*'s assessment or provide further information to justify the invoice already submitted. While the disagreement is being resolved the *Employer* should pay what he considers the proper amount in respect of the *services* provided. This will include substituting his assessment for the *Consultant*'s invoice in respect of that part of the *services* he disagrees with. If he fails to make payment he will be liable to pay interest to the *Consultant* on any delayed payment. (cl 51.4).

51.5 The *interest rate* stated in part one of the Contract Data should comprise a reliable annual base rate applicable to the territory in which the work is to be done plus a percentage (recommended to be at least 2%) to represent the current commercial rates. Simple interest at the *interest rate* applies for periods of less than one year.

Accounts and records **52**

52.1 Appropriate requirements to keep records of *expenses* and Time Charge are stated in the Main Option clauses 52.2 (Option A) and 52.3 (Options C, E and G). Any further requirements for a specific contract should be stated in the Scope.

MAIN OPTION CLAUSES

Option A: Priced contract with activity schedule

The *activity schedule* **53**

53.1 An *activity schedule* which contains items which do not represent the *Consultant*'s proposed activities and methods of working will create difficulties in determining payments due. Thus it is important that the *activity schedule* should relate directly to the programme (also cl 30.3) and always be compatible with it.

53.2 This clause states the reasons which the *Employer* can give for not accepting changes to the *activity schedule* (in addition to non-compliance with the Scope) without creating a compensation event (cl 60.1 (7)). For instance, any change in Prices should not upset the balance of pricing which existed in the original *activity schedule*. The total of the Prices must not be changed except by implemented compensation events.

Option C: Target contract

The *activity schedule* **53**

53.1 It is important that the *activity schedule* should relate directly to the programme and always be compatible with it.

53.2   This clause states the reasons which the *Employer* can give for not accepting changes to the *activity schedule* (in addition to non-compliance with the Scope) without creating a compensation event (cl 60.1(7)). For instance, any change in Prices should not upset the balance of pricing which existed in the original *activity schedule*. The total of the Prices must not be changed except by implemented compensation events.

The *Consultant*'s share   **54**
54.1
54.2

Clause 54.1 states how the *Consultant*'s share is calculated. Clause 54.2 states the main principle of target contracts whereby the *Consultant* receives a share of any saving and pays a share of any excess when the final PSPD (Time Charge) is compared to the target (the total of the Prices).

For example, assume that the Contract Data states that:

- The *Consultant's share percentages* and the *share ranges* are

share range	Consultant's share percentage
less than 80%	15%
from 80% to 90%	30%
from 90% to 110%	50%
greater than 110%	20%

If at Completion of the whole of the *services*, the total of the Prices (having been adjusted for compensation events) is £100K, the Contract Data table becomes in effect:

Final PSPD	Consultant's share percentage
less than £80K	15%
from £80K to £90K	30%
from £90K to £110K	50%
greater than £110K	20%

Examples   Examples of possible outcomes are:

a) Final PSPD = £75K
Saving under total of the Prices = £25K
Comprising 3 increments

less than 80K	= 5K @ 15%	=	0.75K
80K to 90K	= 10K @ 30%	=	3.00K
90K to 110K	= 10K @ 50%	=	5.00K
Consultant's share		=	£8.75K
(paid by *Employer*)			

b) Final PSPD = £95K
Saving under total of the Prices = £5K
Comprising 1 increment

90K to 110K	= 5K @ 50%	=	2.5K
Consultant's share		=	£2.5K
(paid by *Employer*)			

c) Final PSPD = £115K
Excess over total of the Prices = £15K
Comprising 2 increments

90K to 110K	= 10K @ 50%	=	5.0K
greater than 110K	= 5K @ 20%	=	1.0K
Consultant's share		=	£6.0K
(paid to Employer)			

The other potential source of profit for the *Consultant* is within the *staff rates* used to calculate the Time Charge. The *Consultant's share percentages* should be determined in a particular contract to provide the appropriate level of incentive to the *Consultant* to minimise the final PSPD. The extent of financial risk to the Parties in the event of the final PSPD exceeding the total of the Prices, can be varied between two extremes:

- a guaranteed maximum price to the Employer can be achieved by stating the Consultant's share percentage to be 100% above that price:
- a limit to the deduction from the total Time Charge (the final PSPD) paid to the Consultant can be achieved by stating the Consultant's share percentage to be 0% above a stated share range.

Reference should be made to CIRIA Report 85 for further information and guidance on the working of target contracts.

54.3
54.4

Payment of the *Consultant*'s share is made in two stages. Firstly, in the payment due following Completion of the whole of the *services* and secondly in the final payment made after the *defects date*.

Interim payments of the *Consultant*'s share are not provided for. There are two main reasons for this.

- The Prices tendered by a Consultant have the main purpose of establishing the total of the Prices (the target). It is not intended that their build-up should provide a realistic forecast of cash flow. They are therefore unlikely to be comparable with the PSPD at any interim stage.
- Forecasts of both the final PSPD (Time Charge) and the final total of the Prices would be extremely uncertain at early stages of the contract. Any delays in assessing compensation events would further distort the calculation.

The danger of serious under or over payment of an interim *Consultant*'s share has therefore led to the policy of an estimated payment on Completion which is corrected at assessment of the final amount due.

Nevertheless, provision is made in clause 95.5 for the assessment of the *Consultant*'s share if there is a termination.

54.5

This provision is designed to motivate the *Consultant* to investigate and propose changes to the Scope which will reduce the Time Charge. It has the effect of improving the *Consultant*'s share.

Option G: Term contract

Assessing Tasks 55
55.1

The actions to be taken by the *Employer* to initiate the assessment of a proposed Task are stated in this clause.

If all the items in the proposed Task are on the *task schedule*, the *Consultant*'s estimate will be straightforward using the information in the *task schedule* in accordance with clause 55.2. It is therefore most important that the *task schedule* prepared by the *Employer* to be priced by the *Consultant* in his bid, is as comprehensive as possible in the list of items of services which the *Employer* is likely to require to be carried out.

However, if a proposed Task includes items not on the *task schedule*, provision is made for the compensation event assessment procedure (cls 62 and 63) to be used to determine for each item either a lump sum price or that it will be time based. If the *Consultant*'s quotation for the compensation event is accepted by the *Employer*, the new items can be added to the *task schedule* for use in the proposed Task and possible future Tasks.

In this way, the *task schedule* can be developed with the *Employer*'s continuing appreciation of his requirements. However, *Employers* are recommended to anticipate potential new requirements as far ahead as possible so that additions to the *task schedule* can be agreed without undue pressure.

55.2   This clause states how all estimates of the final total of the Prices for a Task are prepared whether by the *Consultant* or the *Employer*. The basis is the *task schedule*, augmented as necessary by new items assessed using the compensation events procedure.

55.3   The estimate must include any quotation for items not on the *task schedule*, assessed as a compensation event. As with all periods in the PSC, the two weeks can be extended by agreement of the Parties.

55.4   This clause states the circumstances in which the *Employer* can assess the final total of the Prices for a Task rather than accept the *Consultant*'s estimate.

55.5   The *Employer* may decide not to proceed with a proposed Task. If he instructs the *Consultant* to carry out the Task he states how it is to be paid for by reference to the *task schedule* (cl 11.2(17)) and *staff rates* as necessary.

6. Compensation events

Compensation events are events stated in the contract which, if they occur, entitle the *Consultant* to be compensated for any effect which the event has on the Prices and on the Accepted Programme (cl 62.2). The assessment of a compensation event is always based on its effect on both the Time Charge and on the Accepted Programme. Compensation events may entitle the *Consultant* to additional payment and possibly additional time in which to carry out the *services*. In some specific cases they may result in a reduced payment to the *Consultant*.

CORE CLAUSES

Compensation events   60.1

Changing the Scope   (1)   Variations to the *services* are effected by an *Employer*'s instruction to change the Scope. The authority given to the *Employer* to make such changes is covered by clause 20.2. A change to the Scope may amend some detail of the *services* to be provided or impose a change in the way the *services* are to be carried out.

When Option G has been chosen the *Employer* should state in his instruction whether a change to the Scope applies generally to the affected items in the *task schedule* or only to the items in a particular Task.

Failure to provide access	(2)	This compensation event arises when the *Employer* fails to provide access in accordance with clause 26.1.
Failure by the *Employer* or Others	(4)	Although the *Consultant* is required to co-operate with Others, if necessary by arranging meetings with them (cls 23.1, 23.2), any failure by them to perform constitutes a compensation event. Thus a failure by a service company not subcontracted to the *Consultant* to provide details of its services in time would constitute a compensation event. The *Employer* will define in the Scope the extent of the interface between the *Consultant* and Others and the extent to which the *Consultant* is entitled to rely upon the performance of Others.
Withholding acceptance	(7)	Various clauses give reasons why the *Employer* may not accept a submission or a proposal from the *Consultant*. Withholding acceptance for any other reason is a compensation event.
Correction of an assumption	(8)	Under clause 61.5 (see later notes) the *Employer* may state assumptions to be used in assessing a compensation event. If he later notifies a correction to these assumptions, the notification is a separate compensation event.
Ambiguities and inconsistencies	(9)	This compensation event relates to clause 16.1, and is based on the "contra preferentem" rule. Thus the *Employer* carries the risk of ambiguities and inconsistencies in documents which he has drafted.
Employer's breach of contract	(10)	This is an "umbrella" clause to include breaches of contract by the *Employer* within the compensation event procedure.
Effect of various events on the *services*	(11)	If any of the listed events occur and affects the *services* causing loss to the *Consultant*, a compensation event occurs. Thus the *Employer* carries the financial risk of these events which are outside the *Consultant*'s control.

Notifying compensation events	**61**	
	61.1	Where the *Employer* issues an instruction changing the Scope he would normally notify the *Consultant* of the compensation event at the same time. If a compensation event arose in any other circumstances, either Party would be free to notify the other. Thus the *Employer* could notify the *Consultant* of a compensation event which he believed should reduce the Prices. The stated time limit for notifying compensation events is intended to expedite the procedure such that dealing with compensation events a long time after they have occurred is avoided.
	61.2	This clause deals with the situation where the *Employer* is considering issuing an instruction or changing a decision but first requires to know what effect this would have on the Prices and the Accepted Programme - for example when he is considering a change to the Scope under clause 60.1(1). He has the authority to instruct the *Consultant* to submit quotations as a first step.
	61.3	This clause lists four tests which the *Employer* applies to an event notified by the *Consultant* in order to decide whether or not to instruct the *Consultant* to submit quotations. If the *Employer* decides that the event does not pass any one of the tests he notifies the *Consultant* and no further action is required unless the *Consultant* disputes the decision and refers it to the *Adjudicator* under clause 90.1.
	61.4	The *Employer* should include in an instruction to submit quotations his decision on whether or not the *Consultant* gave an early warning which an experienced consultant could have given.

35

61.5   In some cases, the nature of the compensation event may be such that it is impossible to prepare a sufficiently accurate quotation. In these cases, quotations are submitted on the basis of assumptions stated by the *Employer* in his instruction to the *Consultant*. If the assumptions later prove to be wrong, the *Employer*'s notification of their correction is a separate compensation event (cl 60.1(8)).

Apart from this situation, the assessment of compensation events cannot be revised (cl 65.2). The reason for this strict procedure is to motivate the Parties to decide the effects of each compensation event either before or soon after it occurs. Since each quotation can include due allowance for risk (cl 63.4) and since the early warning procedure should minimise the effects of unexpected problems, the need for later review is minimal.

Quotations for **62**
compensation events 62.1   There may be several ways of dealing with a compensation event and its consequences. The procedure in this clause enables the *Employer* to consider different options. For instance it may be more beneficial to the *Employer* to have the *services* carried out under the existing programme at a greater cost than an alternative of delaying the *services* but at a lower cost. Quotations include both time and money implications as, in most situations, it is impossible to consider each in isolation.

62.2   Quotations are based on an assessment of Time Charge and time arising from the compensation event. A build-up of each quotation is to be submitted by the *Consultant*. If re-programming of remaining work is affected, the quotation should include a revised programme.

62.3   The time limits are intended to promote efficient management of the contract procedures. The four categories of reply by the *Employer* are listed. The third category may result from the *Employer* deciding not to proceed with a proposed change to the Scope. This may happen when the cost of the change is too high or the delay too great. The *Employer* has absolute discretion in such a case on whether to proceed. The fourth bullet applies when the *Employer* decides that the *Consultant's* quotation is not acceptable.

62.4   This procedure permits revision of quotations. In practice this will usually follow discussion between the *Employer* and the *Consultant* on the details of the submitted quotations. Again, a time limit for submission of the revised quotations is stated.

Assessing compensation **63**
events 63.1   Assessment of compensation events is based entirely on their effect on the Time Charge and time. If some or all of the work arising from a compensation event has already been done, the Time Charge should be readily assessed from records. Forecasting future Time Charges is less straightforward. Estimates of resources and productivity rates are required. For Options C and E, the *Consultant* is paid for the compensation event on an actual time basis. However, the quotations are used for budgeting purposes in providing the forecasts under clause 21.4 and in Option C for changing the total of the Prices to be used in calculating the *Consultant's* share (cl 54).

63.2   No compensation event can result in a reduction in the time for carrying out the *services* i.e. an earlier Completion Date.

The first stage in assessing whether the Completion Date should be delayed as a result of a compensation event is to adjust the programme to take account of the compensation event with any appropriate adjustments to staff time risks allowances (cl 63.4). Any float in the programme before planned Completion is available to mitigate or avoid any consequential delay to planned Completion. If planned Completion is delayed, the Completion Date is delayed by the same period. If planned Completion is not delayed, the Completion Date is not changed.

63.3   The *Consultant*'s duty to give an early warning is stated in clause 15.1. The sanction if the *Consultant* fails to give early warning is stated in this clause. It is possible that early warning could have allowed actions to be taken which would have reduced costs and saved time. It is important that the *Employer* notifies the *Consultant* of his decision that early warning should have been given (cl 61.4) so that the *Consultant* knows the correct basis for his assessment.

63.4   Allowances for staff time risk must be included in forecasts of Time Charge and time. The value of the allowances is greater when the work is uncertain and there is high chance of a *Consultant*'s risk happening. It is least when the uncertainties are small.

63.5   This clause protects the *Employer* against inefficiency on the part of the *Consultant*. The reference to changing the Accepted Programme is made so that it is clear that the *Consultant* is expected to alter his arrangements when necessary.

63.6   It is possible that a compensation event may require some work to be done by a category of person which is not included in the list in Contract Data part two. In this clause the *Consultant* is required to propose staff rates for such people.

63.7   The first of these deductions avoids the *Employer* having to pay for costs which the *Consultant* should have insured against. If the *Consultant* does not insure as required by the contract , such costs are at his own risk. The second deduction makes certain that the *Consultant* does not receive double payment as a result, for example, of insurance which he has voluntarily taken out, or from insuring for a greater cover than required by the contract.

The *Employer*'s   **64**
assessments   64.1   The four circumstances in which the *Employer* assesses a compensation event are stated. The first and third derive from some failure of the *Consultant* to fulfill an obligation under the contract. The second and fourth derive from the *Employer* not accepting a submission from the *Consultant*. The *Employer* is motivated to make a fair and reasonable assessment in the knowledge that the *Consultant* may refer the matter to the *Adjudicator* who may change the assessment.

64.2   This clause states the circumstances in which the *Employer* is to use his own assessment of the programme for the remaining work in his assessment of a compensation event. This is a major incentive for the *Consultant* to keep his programme up to date.

64.3   This clause allows the *Employer* the same time to make his assessment as the *Consultant* was allowed for his.

Implementing **65**
compensation events 65.1   This clause should be read in conjunction with clause 65.3 for option A and C, with clause 65.4 for option E and with clause 65.5 for option G.

Implementation is achieved by the *Employer* changing the Prices and the Completion Date in accordance with the assessment of which he has notified the *Consultant*. In the case of option G, changes to the final total of the Prices and the programme for a Task, are also included.

65.2   This clause emphasises the finality of the assessment of compensation events. If the records of resources on work actually carried out show that actual Time Charge and timing are different from the forecasts included in the accepted quotation or in the *Employer*'s assessment, the assessment is not changed. The only circumstances in which a review is possible are those stated in clause 61.5.

7. Rights to material

CORE CLAUSES

The Parties' use of **70**
material 70.1   Under this clause, the *Consultant* retains rights over material provided by him, but the *Employer* may use them for the purposes stated in the Scope. If option X9 is used, the effect is to transfer these rights to the *Employer* with any exceptions being stated in the Scope. In England and Wales, legal recognition of the right to use material or of the transfer of its ownership can only be achieved if stamped documentary evidence is provided and Stamp Duty is paid.

70.2   The *Consultant* may use any material provided by the *Employer* but this is restricted to the extent necessary to Provide the Services.

70.3   Confidentiality is achieved by the provisions of this clause. The *Consultant* may however publicise certain information provided he obtains the *Employer*'s agreement under clause 71.1.

8. Indemnity, insurance and liability

CORE CLAUSES

Indemnity **80**
80.1   This clause protects the *Employer* in the event that the *Consultant* infringes the rights of Others who may seek redress from the Employer. "Others" are defined in clause 11.2(2). The only exception is when the *Employer* himself provides things for the *Consultant*'s use.

Insurance cover **81**
81.1   Three main types of insurance are required.

    (a)   Professional Indemnity Insurance

        This is the first insurance stated in the Insurance Table, and provides an indemnity in respect of any sum which the *Consultant* may become legally liable to pay arising out of claims made against him during the period of insurance as a result of any neglect error or omission in carrying out his professional activities.

        The amount of cover is to be stated in the Contract Data, and it is for "each claim, without limit to the number of claims". In some circumstances, some insurers decline to insure on this basis and insist on a maximum sum for "any one claim and in the aggregate on the period of insurance".

The period for which insurance cover is required is also to be stated in the Contract Data. Claims in respect of professional indemnity insurance normally have to be made during the period of insurance. Claims cannot normally be made after the period of insurance even though the act of neglect may have taken place during the period of insurance. Thus, in dealing with the period of cover, it is desirable that the policy is kept in force after completion of the services to deal with claims made in respect of negligent acts which do not manifest themselves until some time after. To provide adequate cover in these circumstances, the period stated should be the relevant legal limitation period after Completion.

(b) Public Liability Insurance

This is the second insurance in the Insurance Table and indemnifies the *Consultant* against his legal liability for damages arising from bodily injury to or death of a person (other than the *Consultant*'s employees) or loss of or damage to third party property occurring during the period of insurance. In this type of insurance, the act of neglect leading to liability has to take place during the currency of the policy, but claims can be made afterwards. Hence there is no need to maintain the policy after Completion.

(c) Employer's Liability Insurance

The third insurance in the Insurance Table provides indemnity for legal liability for bodily injury to or death of the *Consultant*'s employees arising out of or in the course of their employment. This insurance is compulsory in the UK, the statutory provisions requiring insurance for a minimum of £2 million for each occurrence. Elsewhere in the world other regulations may apply requiring workmen's compensation-type coverage or participation in state social security schemes. Insurance cover may terminate on Completion.

If the *Employer* provides property for the use of the *Consultant* in providing the *services*, he may require the *Consultant* to insure it for the period during which it is being used by the *Consultant*. Any such requirements should be stated in the Contract Data with cover being for the replacement value of the property.

In some circumstances it may be more appropriate and convenient for the *Employer* to effect some of the *Consultant*'s insurances, for example, by taking out a project insurance policy covering contractors and consultants. In addition, it is likely that other consultants and contractors will be required to carry their own insurances covering certain risks. Where these are relevant to the risks taken by the *Consultant* under this contract, they should be listed in the Contract Data. Examples are contractor's works and third party liability insurances and the *Employer*'s own building insurances.

81.2   Insurers and brokers will generally not release copies of consultants' insurance policies. It is normal however for the *Consultant* to provide a certificate from his broker confirming that he does hold the insurances. In the same way, the *Employer* is required to provide a certificate on request confirming that he holds the necessary insurances.

Limit on the 82
Consultant's **liability** 82.1

The *Consultant's* liability to the *Employer* (i.e. the maximum the *Employer* could recover for the *Consultant's* negligence) will be the amount stated in the Contract Data. This will normally be the amount of the insurance cover. When setting any limit higher than the insurance cover, the consequences on the work of the *Consultant* will need to be recognised (see cl 82.1 and Contract Data under "Optional Statements").

If the *Consultant* is found to be legally liable along with others, the *Consultant's* liability to the *Employer* is limited to his proportionate failure. If, for example, a court were to conclude that a supervisor appointed as a *Consultant* under the Professional Services Contract (PSC) to supervise a construction contract, was 15% liable and the contractor 85% liable for the *Employer's* losses, the maximum the *Employer* could recover from the *Consultant* would be 15% of his losses up to the limit of insurance or other figure stated.

9. Disputes and termination

This section describes the procedure for dealing with disputes and the circumstances under which the Parties may terminate the *Consultant's* appointment and the subsequent procedures.

It is the intention that disputes should be referred to and resolved by the *Adjudicator*. If either Party is dissatisfied with the *Adjudicator's* decision and wishes to pursue the matter further, he is free to refer it to arbitration or the courts, whichever is identified as the *tribunal* in the Contract Data. The Parties may deal with the dispute by other means if they agree to do so.

The following notes on Section 9 apply to the general and international use of the PSC. The key periods affecting dispute procedures are illustrated in Figures 5 and 6, which should be referred to in conjunction with the notes.

In the UK, the Housing Grants, Construction and Regeneration Act 1996 applies to "construction contracts" and "construction operations" as defined in the Act. The core clauses dealing with adjudication do not comply with this Act. Hence for contracts falling within the definition of the Act option Y(UK)2 should be used. Reference should then be made to the separate notes on Option Y(UK)2 which include references to the necessary modifications and additions to core clauses.

NEC Professional Services Contract

Steps in Adjudication for a Disputed Action or Lack of Action on the Part of the *Employer*

Consultant becomes aware of action or lack of action of *Employer*

4 weeks maximum

Consultant notifies *Employer* of dispute

2 weeks minimum
4 weeks maximum

Consultant submits dispute to *Adjudicator* and includes information

4 weeks (or greater agreed period) maximum

Parties may provide *Adjudicator* with further information

4 weeks (or greater agreed period) maximum

Adjudicator notifies Parties of decision with reasons

4 weeks maximum

A Party may notify the other Party of intention to refer dispute to *tribunal*

Tribunal starts proceedings and settles dispute

FIGURE 5

NEC Professional Services Contract

Steps in Adjudication for any other Disputed Matter

Either Party notifies other Party of disputed matter

2 weeks minimum
4 weeks maximum

Either Party submits dispute to *Adjudicator*
and includes information

4 weeks (or greater agreed period) maximum

Parties may provide *Adjudicator* with
further information

4 weeks (or greater agreed period) maximum

Adjudicator notifies Parties of decision
with reasons

4 weeks maximum

A Party may notify the other Party of intention to
refer dispute to *tribunal*

Tribunal starts proceedings and settles
dispute

FIGURE 6

CORE CLAUSES

Adjudication of disputes   **90**

90.1   This clause requires that any disputed action or inaction of the *Employer* or any other disputed matter is submitted to the *Adjudicator*. Time limits are provided for notification of the dispute to the other Party and for submission to the *Adjudicator*.

The person appointed as *Adjudicator* is named in part one of the Contract Data. Normally he will be appointed jointly by the Parties using the NEC Adjudicator's Contract (one of the documents of the NEC family of standard contracts published by Thomas Telford, London) under which the Parties indemnify him against third party claims. Also his fees and expenses are shared equally between the Parties to a dispute, regardless of his decision, unless otherwise agreed.

The *Adjudicator* should be a person with experience of the kind of *services* required of the *Consultant* and who occupies or has occupied a senior position dealing with similar dispute problems. He should be able to understand the point of view of both *Employer* and *Consultant,* to judge the required level of skill and care and be able to act impartially and in a spirit of independence.

90.2   The *Adjudicator* in notifying his decision is required to state reasons for his decision and also to include his assessment of additional cost and delay as appropriate (cl 92.1). Pending settlement of the dispute, the Parties proceed with their duties under the contract.

The adjudication   **91**

91.1   It is important that the *Adjudicator* has all the relevant information to enable him to reach a decision. The Parties are required to submit all information supporting their case within four weeks of the first submission to the *Adjudicator*. The *Adjudicator* must then notify his decision within four weeks of the end of the period for providing information.

In complex disputes and for other valid reasons the *Adjudicator* may require a period greater than the four weeks stated. An extension of the period requires the agreement of the Parties. If such agreement is not forthcoming and the *Adjudicator* cannot, or for some other reason does not notify his decision within the four week period, either Party may refer the dispute to the *tribunal* under clause 93.1.

91.2   Where a dispute which affects services being carried out by a Subconsultant arises and which may constitute a dispute between the *Consultant* and the Subconsultant as well as between the *Consultant* and the *Employer*, there is provision for the matter to be resolved between the three Parties by the *Adjudicator* named in this contract. This prevents the dispute being dealt with by different adjudicators who may make different decisions. This does mean, however, that the adjudicator named in the subcontract will not be used for the dispute under that subcontract, and the Subconsultant will be obliged to use an *Adjudicator* he has not previously agreed to. It would be helpful if the *Adjudicator*'s name is included in the subconsultancy contract documents so that Subconsultants have prior knowledge of the identity of the *Adjudicator* in the main contract.

91.3   A *Consultant* may be appointed under a subcontract using the PSC (see Appendix 3). An example is where the *Consultant* is appointed by a *Contractor* to do design for him in a main contract. This clause permits any dispute which may arise between the Parties of the PSC (the *Employer* being the *Contractor* in the main contract in the above example) to be resolved by the *Adjudicator* named in the main contract provided that the dispute also constitutes a dispute under the main contract and that the main contract permits joint adjudication. This saves time and expense and avoids a situation where a dispute may be dealt with by two adjudicators, with a possibility of different decisions.

The *Adjudicator*   92

92.1   Although the *Adjudicator* is empowered to review and revise any action or inaction of the *Employer*, the Parties are not permitted to widen the dispute to include other disputes which might have occurred after the original submission. It is important that copies of the communications sent to the *Adjudicator* are sent to the other Party so that each Party is aware of the other Party's case.

92.2   This clause provides for the appointment of a replacement adjudicator in the event that the *Adjudicator's* appointment is terminated. Any existing disputes on which the original *Adjudicator* has not made a decision are automatically referred to the replacement Adjudicator. It is important that the Parties ensure that the replacement adjudicator receives all the relevant information. The time stated in the contract for supply of information then runs from the time of appointment of the replacement Adjudicator.

If a need arises for a temporary replacement adjudicator (e.g. during the *Adjudicator's* holiday) the Parties should agree a temporary appointment.

Review by the *tribunal*   93

93.1   Initially the *Employer*, and by acceptance also the *Consultant* and Sub-Consultant, will select the method of final and binding dispute resolution. It can be either arbitration or litigation in the appropriate court.

If arbitration is chosen, the entry in the Contract Data against the *tribunal* is "arbitration" together with the arbitration procedure proposed for the conduct of the arbitration.

If litigation is chosen, appropriate entries must be made for the jurisdiction chosen. In England and Wales, the *tribunal* might be "trial by a judge sitting as such in the High Court of Justice in London". Advice should be taken, however, on the appropriate entry to provide for the jurisdiction intended.

A dispute cannot be referred to arbitration or litigation unless it has first been referred to the *Adjudicator*. A time limit is given for notification of intention to refer the matter to the *tribunal*, after which the Adjudicator's decision will be final and no further notification of intended reference to the *tribunal* may be made. If the adjudication involves three Parties - i.e. a subconsultant is joined in the adjudication - the dispute resolution by the *tribunal* will also involve all three parties.

Termination 94

94.1 to .3 Both the *Employer* and the *Consultant* have limited rights of termination of appointment of the *Consultant* under the core clauses. The *Employer* effectively may terminate whenever he no longer requires the *services*. He may also terminate if a *Consultant* is substantially in breach of contract. The *Consultant* may terminate if a payment has not been made within 11 weeks after serving a notice that payment is overdue.

In any event either Party may terminate on the insolvency of the other. The terms used in clause 94.1 for insolvency are those current in English law, but the clause allows for their equivalent in other jurisdictions.

Secondary Option X11 provides for termination at will by the *Employer* (see Guidance Note on Option X11).

Procedures and 95
payment after 95.1 This clause covers the work required following termination to achieve an
termination orderly close-down of the *Consultant*'s *services*. It includes for the assignment of a subconsultancy, but it should be recognised that the co-operation of the Subconsultant would be required to complete the *services* satisfactorily.

After termination, the *Consultant* must hand over to the *Employer* all material he was preparing for him under the contract, but the *Consultant* is entitled to keep the material until he has been paid. Any dispute over the amount of the final payment would be subject to adjudication.

95.2
95.3 These clauses set out how the final payment from the *Employer* to the *Consultant* is assessed following termination. The *Consultant* is paid the amount he was already due plus any retentions and other costs to which he is committed . If the termination is due to the insolvency or default of the *Consultant*, the *Employer* is entitled to deduct from those costs the forecast additional cost to him of completing the *services* (cl 95.3). This would include the costs of appointing a replacement consultant.

MAIN OPTION CLAUSES

Option C: Target contract

Procedures and 95
payment after 95.5 Following termination of an option C target contract, the *Consultant*'s
termination share is assessed at that time in accordance with clause 54 using the Price for Services Provided to Date at termination and the total of the Prices for the work done as set out in the *activity schedule.*

The Institution of Civil Engineers

Flow charts for

The Professional Services Contract

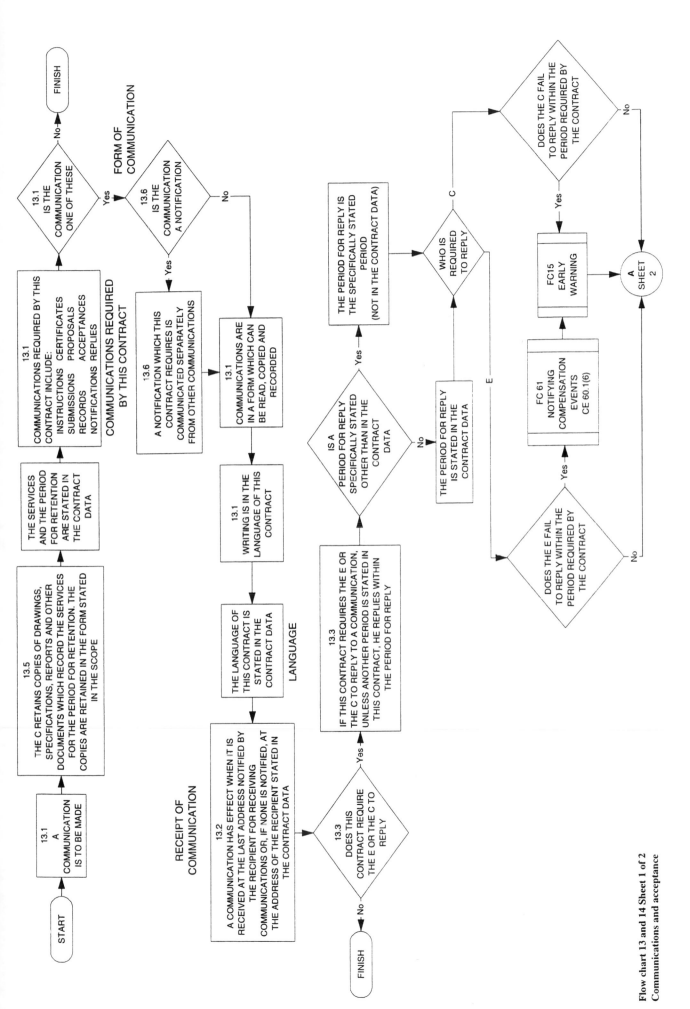

Flow chart 13 and 14 Sheet 1 of 2
Communications and acceptance

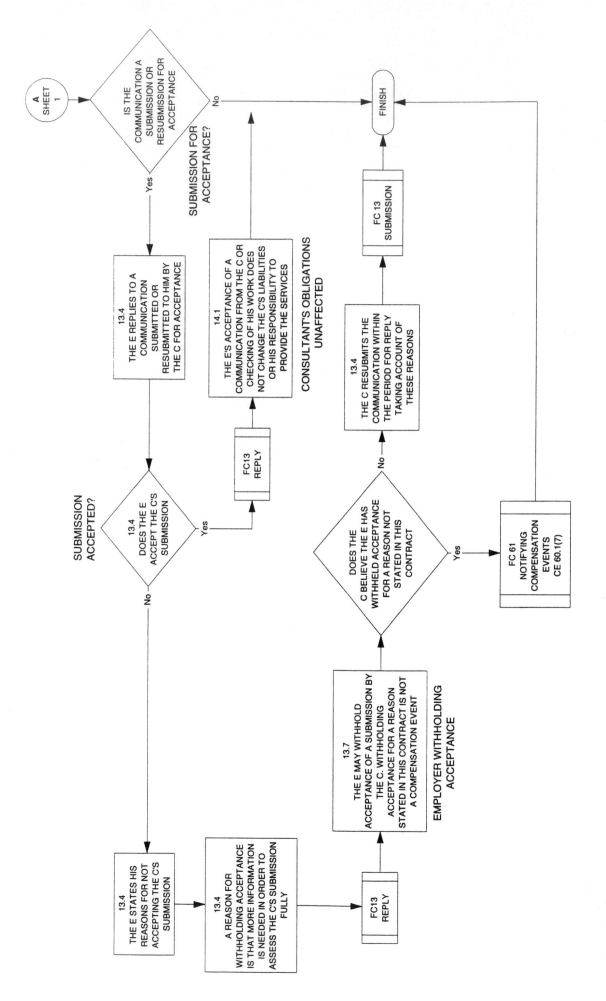

Flow chart 13 and 14 Sheet 2 of 2
Communications and acceptance

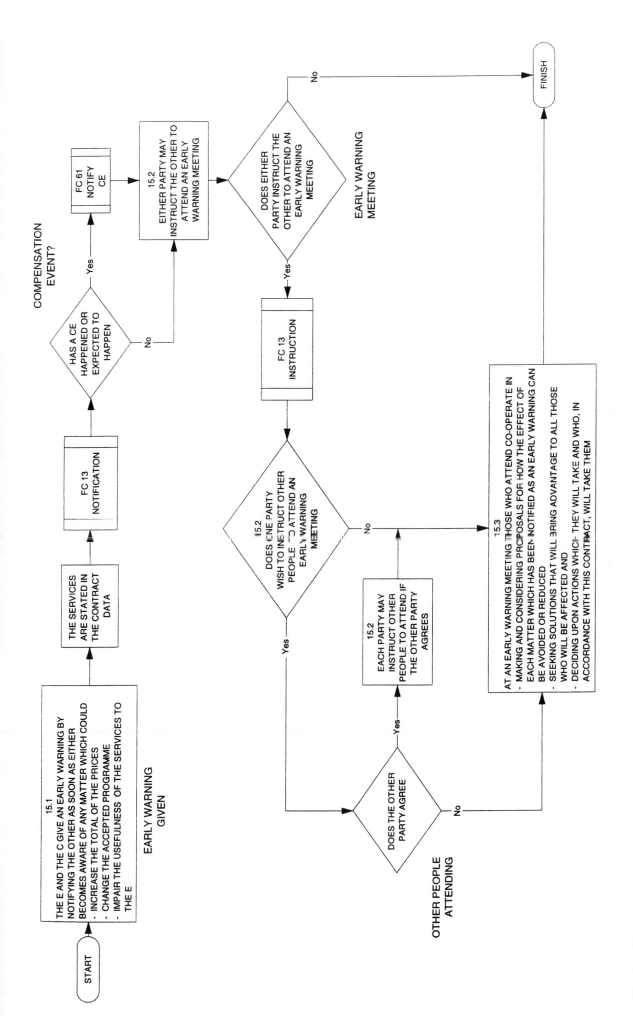

COMPENSATION
EVENT?

15.1
THE E AND THE C GIVE AN EARLY WARNING BY
NOTIFYING THE OTHER AS SOON AS EITHER
BECOMES AWARE OF ANY MATTER WHICH COULD
- INCREASE THE TOTAL OF THE PRICES
- CHANGE THE ACCEPTED PROGRAMME
- IMPAIR THE USEFULNESS OF THE SERVICES TO
THE E

EARLY WARNING
GIVEN

THE SERVICES
ARE STATED IN
THE CONTRACT
DATA

FC 13
NOTIFICATION

HAS A CE
HAPPENED OR
EXPECTED TO
HAPPEN

Yes

No

FC 61
NOTIFY
CE

15.2
EITHER PARTY MAY
INSTRUCT THE OTHER TO
ATTEND AN EARLY
WARNING MEETING

DOES EITHER
PARTY INSTRUCT THE
OTHER TO ATTEND AN
EARLY WARNING
MEETING

EARLY WARNING
MEETING

No

Yes

FC 13
INSTRUCTION

15.2
DOES ONE PARTY
WISH TO INSTRUCT OTHER
PEOPLE TO ATTEND AN
EARLY WARNING
MEETING

Yes

No

15.2
EACH PARTY MAY
INSTRUCT OTHER
PEOPLE TO ATTEND IF
THE OTHER PARTY
AGREES

DOES THE OTHER
PARTY AGREE

Yes

No

OTHER PEOPLE
ATTENDING

15.3
AT AN EARLY WARNING MEETING THOSE WHO ATTEND CO-OPERATE IN
- MAKING AND CONSIDERING PROPOSALS FOR HOW THE EFFECT OF
  EACH MATTER WHICH HAS BEEN NOTIFIED AS AN EARLY WARNING CAN
  BE AVOIDED OR REDUCED
- SEEKING SOLUTIONS THAT WILL BRING ADVANTAGE TO ALL THOSE
  WHO WILL BE AFFECTED AND
- DECIDING UPON ACTIONS WHICH THEY WILL TAKE AND WHO, IN
  ACCORDANCE WITH THIS CONTRACT, WILL TAKE THEM

START

FINISH

Flow chart 15
Early warning

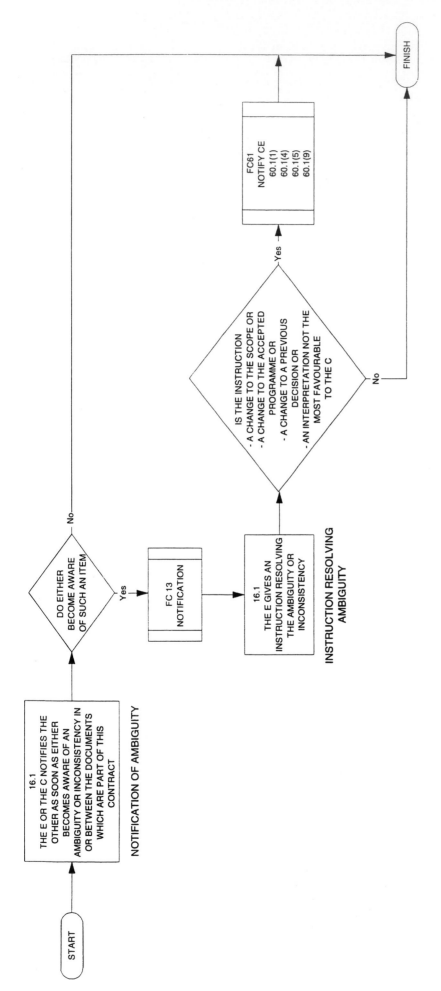

Flow chart 16

Ambiguities and inconsistencies

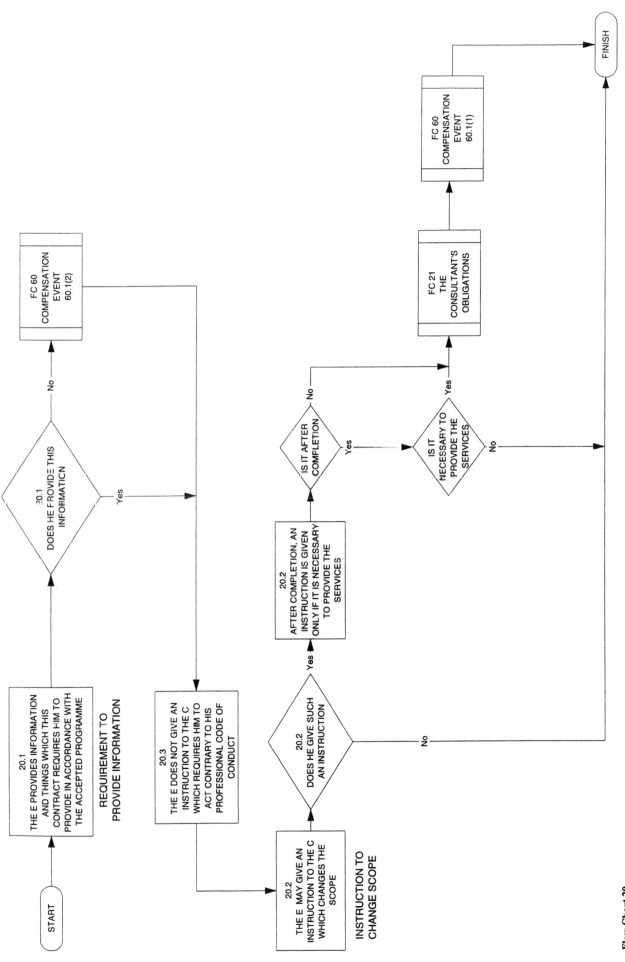

START

20.1
THE E PROVIDES INFORMATION AND THINGS WHICH THIS CONTRACT REQUIRES HIM TO PROVIDE IN ACCORDANCE WITH THE ACCEPTED PROGRAMME

REQUIREMENT TO PROVIDE INFORMATION

20.1
DOES HE PROVIDE THIS INFORMATION

No → FC 60 COMPENSATION EVENT 60.1(2)

Yes

20.3
THE E DOES NOT GIVE AN INSTRUCTION TO THE C WHICH REQUIRES HIM TO ACT CONTRARY TO HIS PROFESSIONAL CODE OF CONDUCT

20.2
THE E MAY GIVE AN INSTRUCTION TO THE C WHICH CHANGES THE SCOPE

INSTRUCTION TO CHANGE SCOPE

20.2
DOES HE GIVE SUCH AN INSTRUCTION

No

Yes

20.2
AFTER COMPLETION, AN INSTRUCTION IS GIVEN ONLY IF IT IS NECESSARY TO PROVIDE THE SERVICES

IS IT AFTER COMPLETION

No → FC 21 THE CONSULTANT'S OBLIGATIONS → FC 60 COMPENSATION EVENT 60.1(1) → FINISH

Yes

IS IT NECESSARY TO PROVIDE THE SERVICES

Yes

No

Flow Chart 20
The *Employer's* obligations

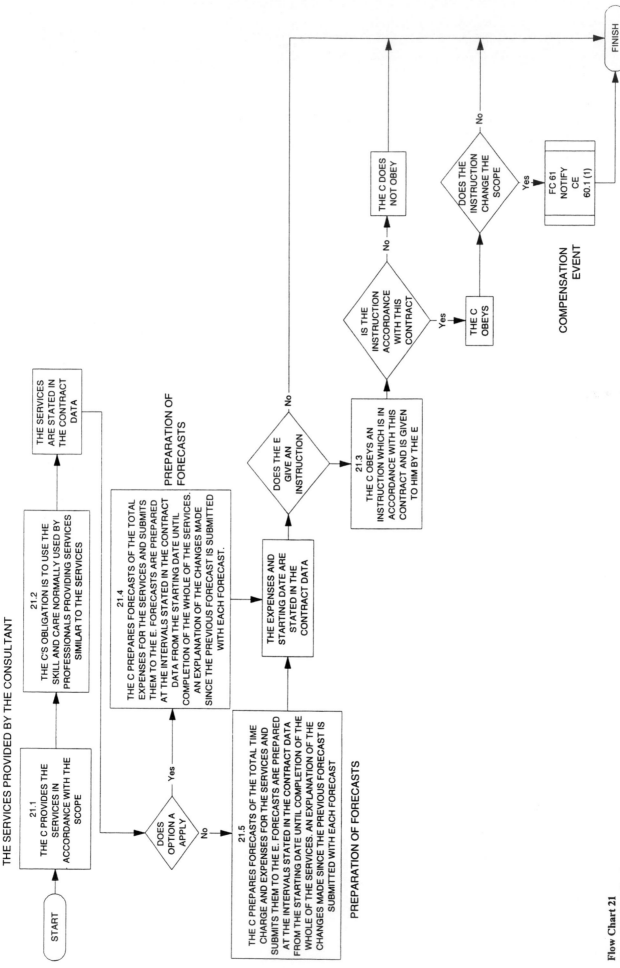

THE SERVICES PROVIDED BY THE CONSULTANT

START

21.1
THE C PROVIDES THE SERVICES IN ACCORDANCE WITH THE SCOPE

21.2
THE C'S OBLIGATION IS TO USE THE SKILL AND CARE NORMALLY USED BY PROFESSIONALS PROVIDING SERVICES SIMILAR TO THE SERVICES

THE SERVICES ARE STATED IN THE CONTRACT DATA

DOES OPTION A APPLY

Yes

21.4
THE C PREPARES FORECASTS OF THE TOTAL EXPENSES FOR THE SERVICES AND SUBMITS THEM TO THE E. FORECASTS ARE PREPARED AT THE INTERVALS STATED IN THE CONTRACT DATA FROM THE STARTING DATE UNTIL COMPLETION OF THE WHOLE OF THE SERVICES. AN EXPLANATION OF THE CHANGES MADE SINCE THE PREVIOUS FORECAST IS SUBMITTED WITH EACH FORECAST.

PREPARATION OF FORECASTS

No

21.5
THE C PREPARES FORECASTS OF THE TOTAL TIME CHARGE AND EXPENSES FOR THE SERVICES AND SUBMITS THEM TO THE E. FORECASTS ARE PREPARED AT THE INTERVALS STATED IN THE CONTRACT DATA FROM THE STARTING DATE UNTIL COMPLETION OF THE WHOLE OF THE SERVICES. AN EXPLANATION OF THE CHANGES MADE SINCE THE PREVIOUS FORECAST IS SUBMITTED WITH EACH FORECAST

PREPARATION OF FORECASTS

THE EXPENSES AND STARTING DATE ARE STATED IN THE CONTRACT DATA

DOES THE E GIVE AN INSTRUCTION

No

21.3
THE C OBEYS AN INSTRUCTION WHICH IS IN ACCORDANCE WITH THIS CONTRACT AND IS GIVEN TO HIM BY THE E

IS THE INSTRUCTION ACCORDANCE WITH THIS CONTRACT

No

THE C DOES NOT OBEY

Yes

THE C OBEYS

DOES THE INSTRUCTION CHANGE THE SCOPE

No

Yes

FC 61 NOTIFY CE 60.1 (1)

COMPENSATION EVENT

FINISH

Flow Chart 21
Consultant's obligations

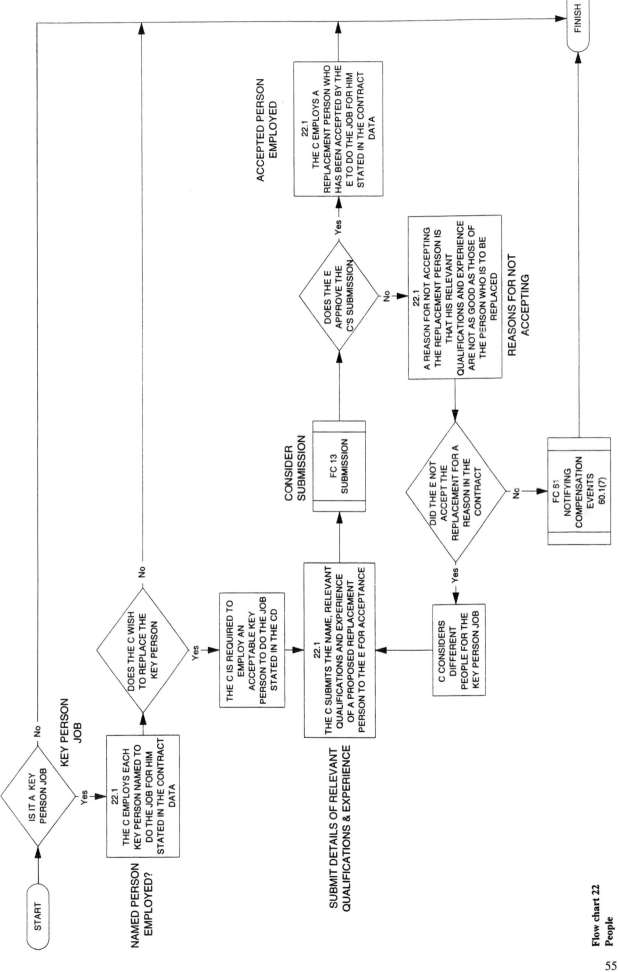

FINISH

ACCEPTED PERSON EMPLOYED

22.1
THE C EMPLOYS A REPLACEMENT PERSON WHO HAS BEEN ACCEPTED BY THE E TO DO THE JOB FOR HIM STATED IN THE CONTRACT DATA

DOES THE E APPROVE THE C'S SUBMISSION — Yes

No

22.1
A REASON FOR NOT ACCEPTING THE REPLACEMENT PERSON IS THAT HIS RELEVANT QUALIFICATIONS AND EXPERIENCE ARE NOT AS GOOD AS THOSE OF THE PERSON WHO IS TO BE REPLACED

REASONS FOR NOT ACCEPTING

CONSIDER SUBMISSION

FC 13
SUBMISSION

DID THE E NOT ACCEPT THE REPLACEMENT FOR A REASON IN THE CONTRACT — No

Yes

FC 61
NOTIFYING COMPENSATION EVENTS
60.1(7)

KEY PERSON JOB

No

DOES THE C WISH TO REPLACE THE KEY PERSON — Yes

THE C IS REQUIRED TO EMPLOY AN ACCEPTABLE KEY PERSON TO DO THE JOB STATED IN THE CD

22.1
THE C SUBMITS THE NAME, RELEVANT QUALIFICATIONS AND EXPERIENCE OF A PROPOSED REPLACEMENT PERSON TO THE E FOR ACCEPTANCE

C CONSIDERS DIFFERENT PEOPLE FOR THE KEY PERSON JOB

NAMED PERSON EMPLOYED?

IS IT A KEY PERSON JOB — No

Yes

22.1
THE C EMPLOYS EACH KEY PERSON NAMED TO DO THE JOB FOR HIM STATED IN THE CONTRACT DATA

START

SUBMIT DETAILS OF RELEVANT QUALIFICATIONS & EXPERIENCE

Flow chart 22
People

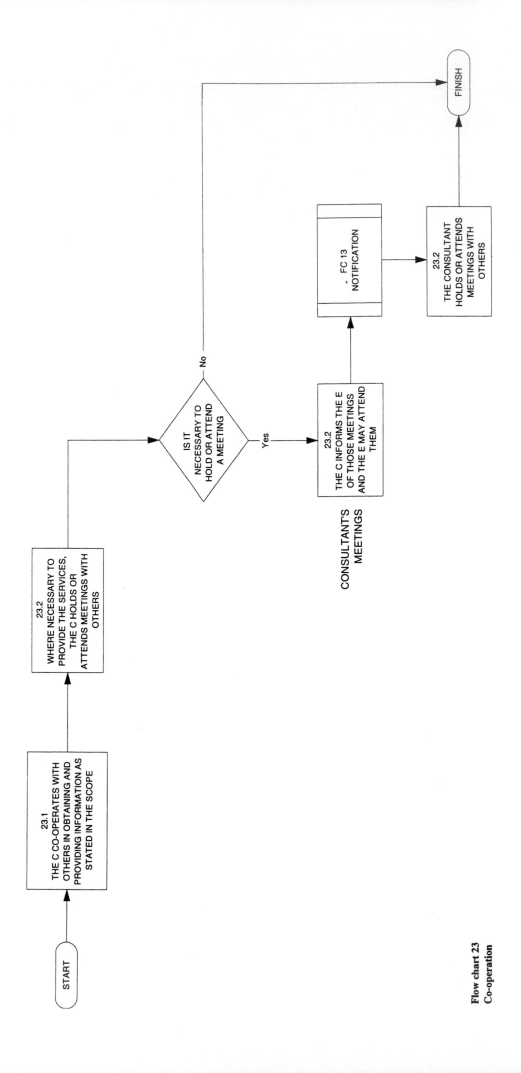

START

23.1
THE C CO-OPERATES WITH OTHERS IN OBTAINING AND PROVIDING INFORMATION AS STATED IN THE SCOPE

23.2
WHERE NECESSARY TO PROVIDE THE SERVICES, THE C HOLDS OR ATTENDS MEETINGS WITH OTHERS

IS IT NECESSARY TO HOLD OR ATTEND A MEETING

No

Yes

CONSULTANT'S MEETINGS

23.2
THE C INFORMS THE E OF THOSE MEETINGS AND THE E MAY ATTEND THEM

FC 13
NOTIFICATION

23.2
THE CONSULTANT HOLDS OR ATTENDS MEETINGS WITH OTHERS

FINISH

Flow chart 23
Co-operation

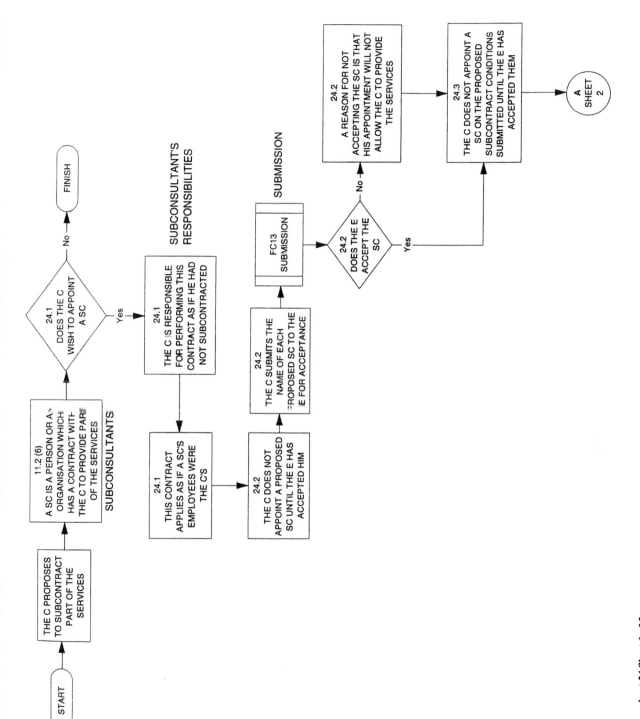

Flow chart 24 Sheet 1 of 2
Subconsulting

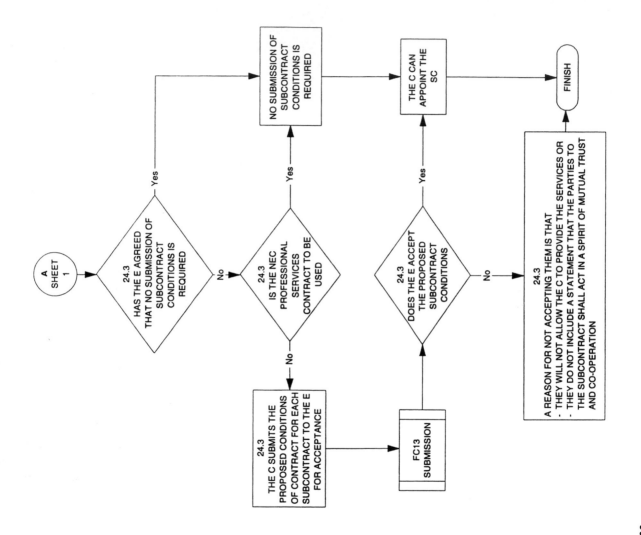

Flow chart 24 Sheet 2 of 2
Subconsulting

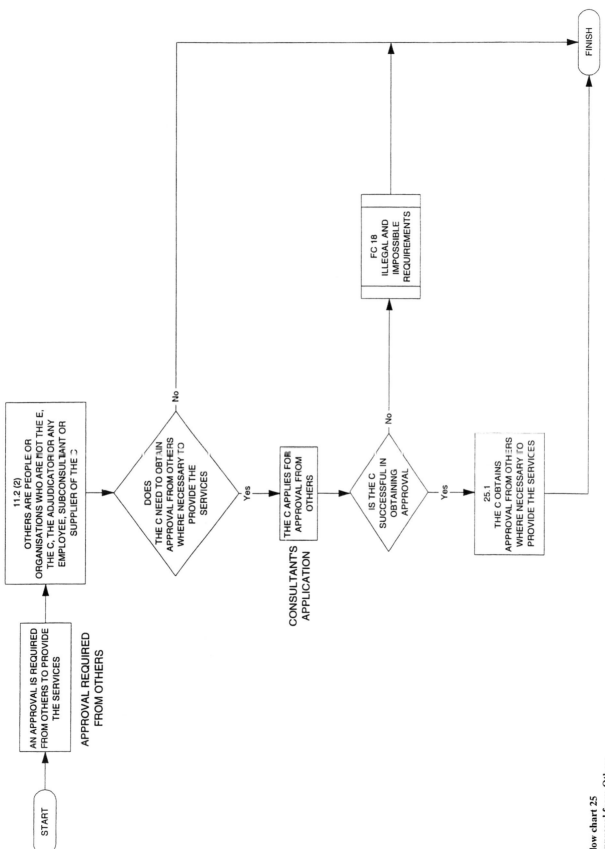

START

AN APPROVAL IS REQUIRED
FROM OTHERS TO PROVIDE
THE SERVICES

APPROVAL REQUIRED
FROM OTHERS

11.2 (2)
OTHERS ARE PEOPLE OR
ORGANISATIONS WHO ARE NOT THE E,
THE C, THE ADJUDICATOR OR ANY
EMPLOYEE, SUBCONSULTANT OR
SUPPLIER OF THE C

DOES
THE C NEED TO OBTAIN
APPROVAL FROM OTHERS
WHERE NECESSARY TO
PROVIDE THE
SERVICES

No

Yes

THE C APPLIES FOR
APPROVAL FROM
OTHERS

CONSULTANT'S
APPLICATION

IS THE C
SUCCESSFUL IN
OBTAINING
APPROVAL

No

Yes

FC 18
ILLEGAL AND
IMPOSSIBLE
REQUIREMENTS

25.1
THE C OBTAINS
APPROVAL FROM OTHERS
WHERE NECESSARY TO
PROVIDE THE SERVICES

FINISH

Flow chart 25
Approval from Others

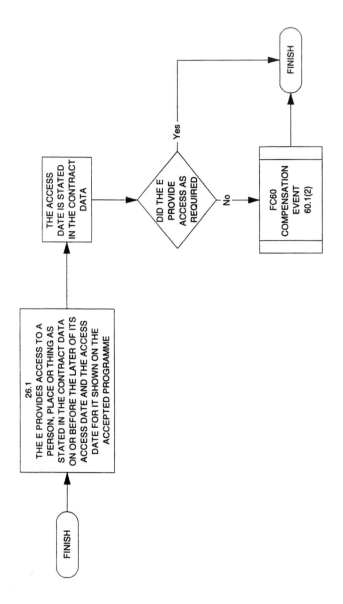

Flow chart 26
Access

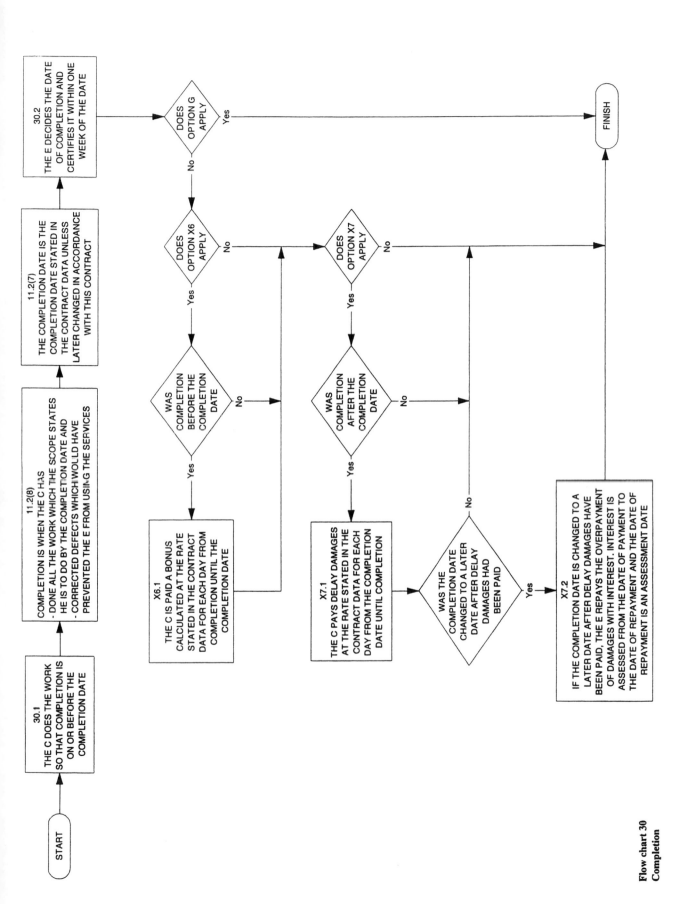

Flow chart 30
Completion

START

30.1
THE C DOES THE WORK SO THAT COMPLETION IS ON OR BEFORE THE COMPLETION DATE

11.2(8)
COMPLETION IS WHEN THE C HAS
- DONE ALL THE WORK WHICH THE SCOPE STATES HE IS TO DO BY THE COMPLETION DATE AND
- CORRECTED DEFECTS WHICH WOULD HAVE PREVENTED THE E FROM USING THE SERVICES

11.2(7)
THE COMPLETION DATE IS THE COMPLETION DATE STATED IN THE CONTRACT DATA UNLESS LATER CHANGED IN ACCORDANCE WITH THIS CONTRACT

30.2
THE E DECIDES THE DATE OF COMPLETION AND CERTIFIES IT WITHIN ONE WEEK OF THE DATE

DOES OPTION G APPLY — Yes → FINISH

No

DOES OPTION X6 APPLY

Yes → WAS COMPLETION BEFORE THE COMPLETION DATE

Yes → **X6.1** THE C IS PAID A BONUS CALCULATED AT THE RATE STATED IN THE CONTRACT DATA FOR EACH DAY FROM COMPLETION UNTIL THE COMPLETION DATE

No

No → DOES OPTION X7 APPLY

Yes → WAS COMPLETION AFTER THE COMPLETION DATE

Yes → **X7.1** THE C PAYS DELAY DAMAGES AT THE RATE STATED IN THE CONTRACT DATA FOR EACH DAY FROM THE COMPLETION DATE UNTIL COMPLETION

No

WAS THE COMPLETION DATE CHANGED TO A LATER DATE AFTER DELAY DAMAGES HAD BEEN PAID

No

Yes → **X7.2** IF THE COMPLETION DATE IS CHANGED TO A LATER DATE AFTER DELAY DAMAGES HAVE BEEN PAID, THE E REPAYS THE OVERPAYMENT OF DAMAGES WITH INTEREST. INTEREST IS ASSESSED FROM THE DATE OF PAYMENT TO THE DATE OF REPAYMENT AND THE DATE OF REPAYMENT IS AN ASSESSMENT DATE

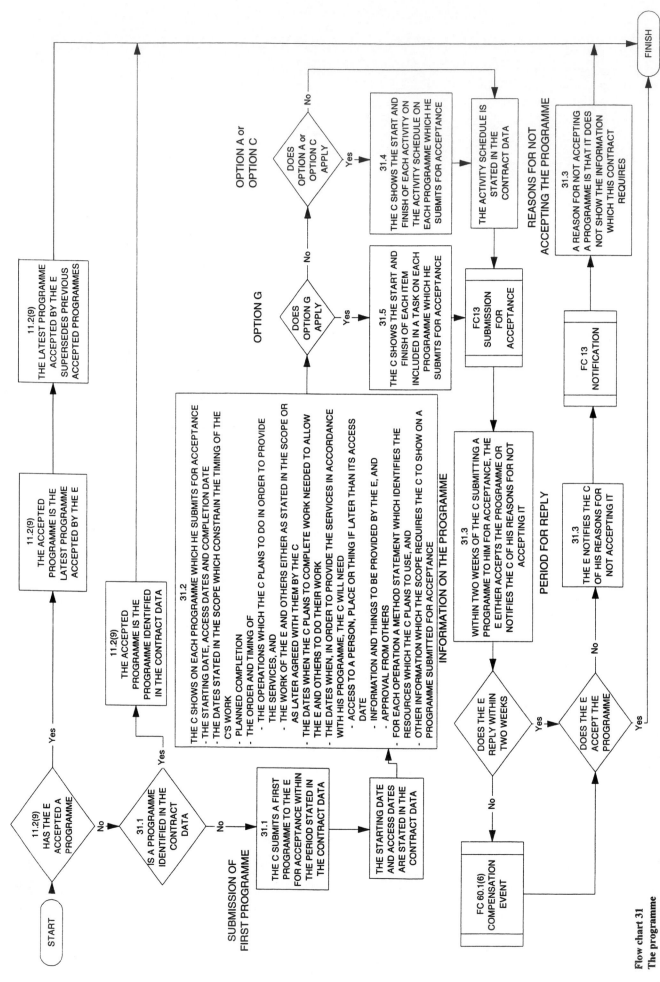

Flow chart 31
The programme

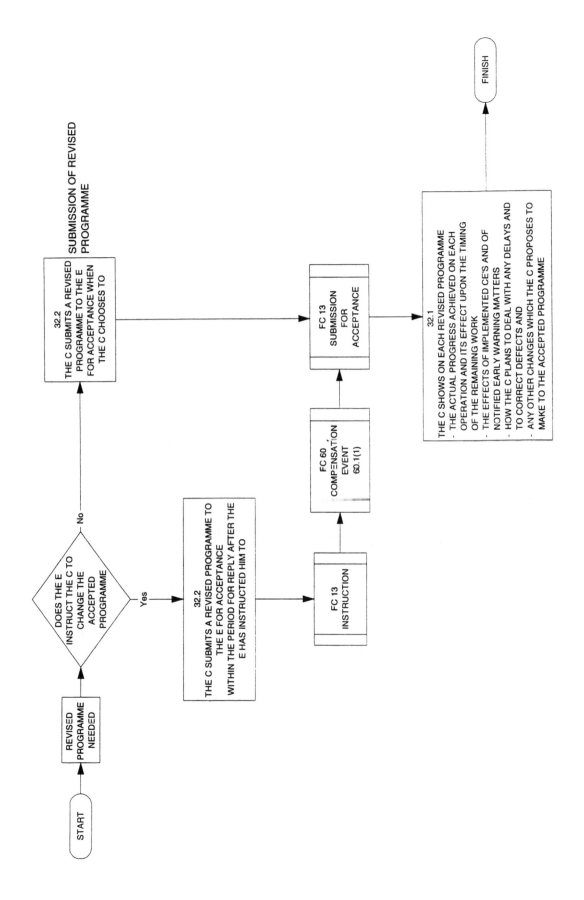

SUBMISSION OF REVISED PROGRAMME

START

REVISED PROGRAMME NEEDED

DOES THE E INSTRUCT THE C TO CHANGE THE ACCEPTED PROGRAMME

No

Yes

32.2
THE C SUBMITS A REVISED PROGRAMME TO THE E FOR ACCEPTANCE WHEN THE C CHOOSES TO

32.2
THE C SUBMITS A REVISED PROGRAMME TO THE E FOR ACCEPTANCE WITHIN THE PERIOD FOR REPLY AFTER THE E HAS INSTRUCTED HIM TO

FC 13
INSTRUCTION

FC 60
COMPENSATION EVENT 60.1(1)

FC 13
SUBMISSION FOR ACCEPTANCE

32.1
THE C SHOWS ON EACH REVISED PROGRAMME
- THE ACTUAL PROGRESS ACHIEVED ON EACH OPERATION AND ITS EFFECT UPON THE TIMING OF THE REMAINING WORK
- THE EFFECTS OF IMPLEMENTED CE'S AND OF NOTIFIED EARLY WARNING MATTERS
- HOW THE C PLANS TO DEAL WITH ANY DELAYS AND TO CORRECT DEFECTS AND
- ANY OTHER CHANGES WHICH THE C PROPOSES TO MAKE TO THE ACCEPTED PROGRAMME

FINISH

Flow chart 32
Revising the programme

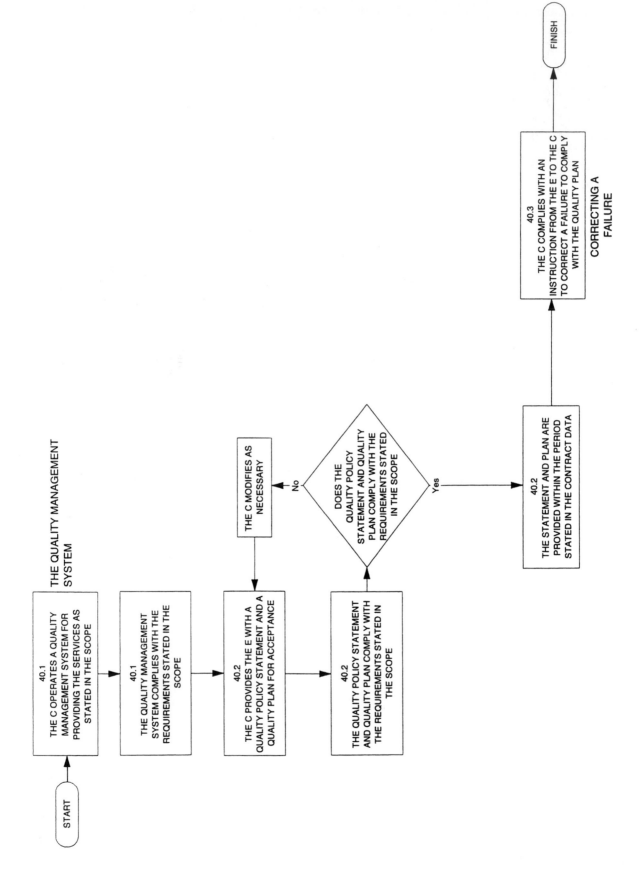

THE QUALITY MANAGEMENT SYSTEM

START

40.1
THE C OPERATES A QUALITY MANAGEMENT SYSTEM FOR PROVIDING THE SERVICES AS STATED IN THE SCOPE

40.1
THE QUALITY MANAGEMENT SYSTEM COMPLIES WITH THE REQUIREMENTS STATED IN THE SCOPE

40.2
THE C PROVIDES THE E WITH A QUALITY POLICY STATEMENT AND A QUALITY PLAN FOR ACCEPTANCE

THE C MODIFIES AS NECESSARY

40.2
THE QUALITY POLICY STATEMENT AND QUALITY PLAN COMPLY WITH THE REQUIREMENTS STATED IN THE SCOPE

DOES THE QUALITY POLICY STATEMENT AND QUALITY PLAN COMPLY WITH THE REQUIREMENTS STATED IN THE SCOPE

No

Yes

40.2
THE STATEMENT AND PLAN ARE PROVIDED WITHIN THE PERIOD STATED IN THE CONTRACT DATA

40.3
THE C COMPLIES WITH AN INSTRUCTION FROM THE E TO THE C TO CORRECT A FAILURE TO COMPLY WITH THE QUALITY PLAN

CORRECTING A FAILURE

FINISH

Flow chart 40
Quality management system

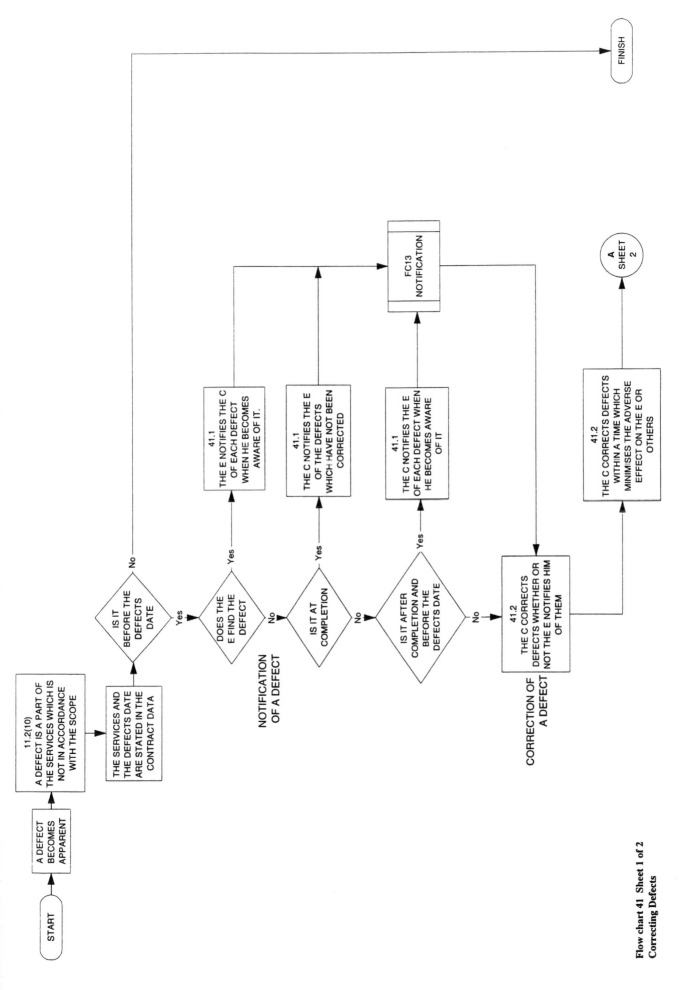

Flow chart 41 Sheet 1 of 2
Correcting Defects

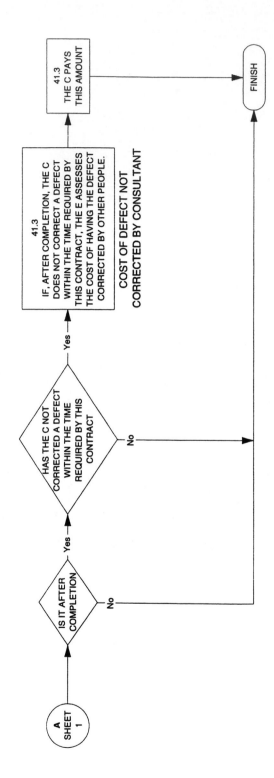

Flow chart 41 Sheet 2 of 2
Correcting Defects

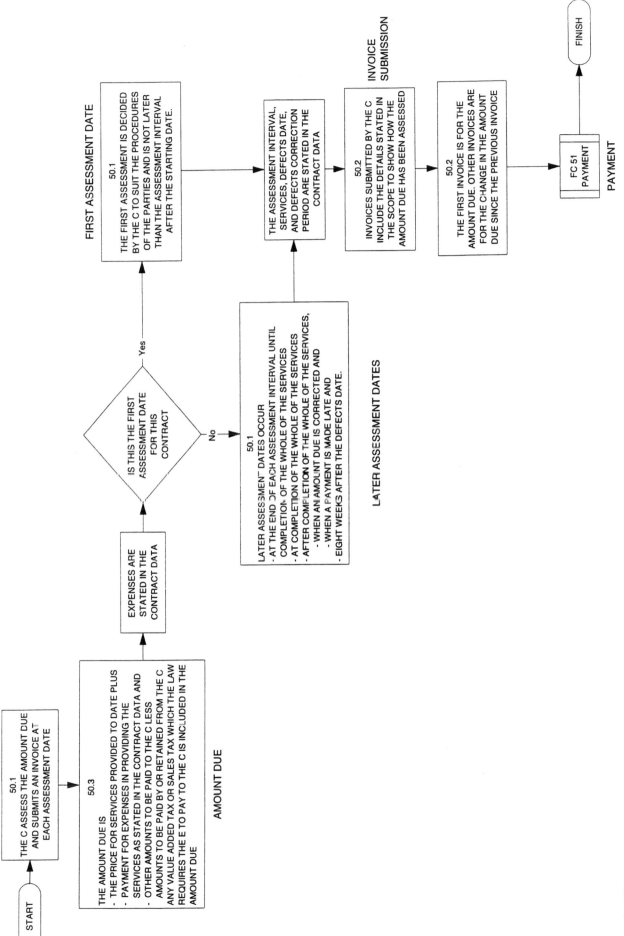

START

50.1
THE C ASSESS THE AMOUNT DUE AND SUBMITS AN INVOICE AT EACH ASSESSMENT DATE

50.3
THE AMOUNT DUE IS
- THE PRICE FOR SERVICES PROVIDED TO DATE PLUS
- PAYMENT FOR EXPENSES IN PROVIDING THE SERVICES AS STATED IN THE CONTRACT DATA AND
- OTHER AMOUNTS TO BE PAID TO THE C LESS
AMOUNTS TO BE PAID BY OR RETAINED FROM THE C
ANY VALUE ADDED TAX OR SALES TAX WHICH THE LAW REQUIRES THE E TO PAY TO THE C IS INCLUDED IN THE AMOUNT DUE

AMOUNT DUE

EXPENSES ARE STATED IN THE CONTRACT DATA

IS THIS THE FIRST ASSESSMENT DATE FOR THIS CONTRACT

Yes

No

50.1
LATER ASSESSMENT DATES OCCUR
- AT THE END OF EACH ASSESSMENT INTERVAL UNTIL COMPLETION OF THE WHOLE OF THE SERVICES
- AT COMPLETION OF THE WHOLE OF THE SERVICES
- AFTER COMPLETION OF THE WHOLE OF THE SERVICES,
  - WHEN AN AMOUNT DUE IS CORRECTED AND
  - WHEN A PAYMENT IS MADE LATE AND
  - EIGHT WEEKS AFTER THE DEFECTS DATE.

LATER ASSESSMENT DATES

FIRST ASSESSMENT DATE

50.1
THE FIRST ASSESSMENT IS DECIDED BY THE C TO SUIT THE PROCEDURES OF THE PARTIES AND IS NOT LATER THAN THE ASSESSMENT INTERVAL AFTER THE STARTING DATE.

THE ASSESSMENT INTERVAL, SERVICES, DEFECTS DATE, AND DEFECTS CORRECTION PERIOD ARE STATED IN THE CONTRACT DATA

INVOICE SUBMISSION

50.2
INVOICES SUBMITTED BY THE C INCLUDE THE DETAILS STATED IN THE SCOPE TO SHOW HOW THE AMOUNT DUE HAS BEEN ASSESSED

50.2
THE FIRST INVOICE IS FOR THE AMOUNT DUE. OTHER INVOICES ARE FOR THE CHANGE IN THE AMOUNT DUE SINCE THE PREVIOUS INVOICE

FC 51
PAYMENT

PAYMENT

FINISH

Flow chart 50
Assessing the amount due

67

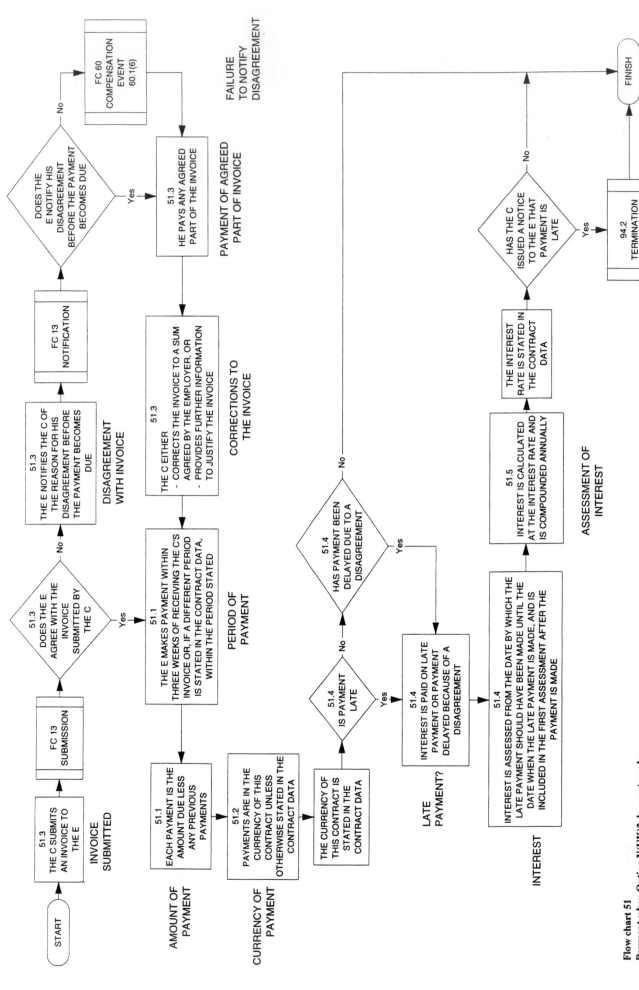

Flow chart 51
Payment when Option Y(UK)2 does not apply

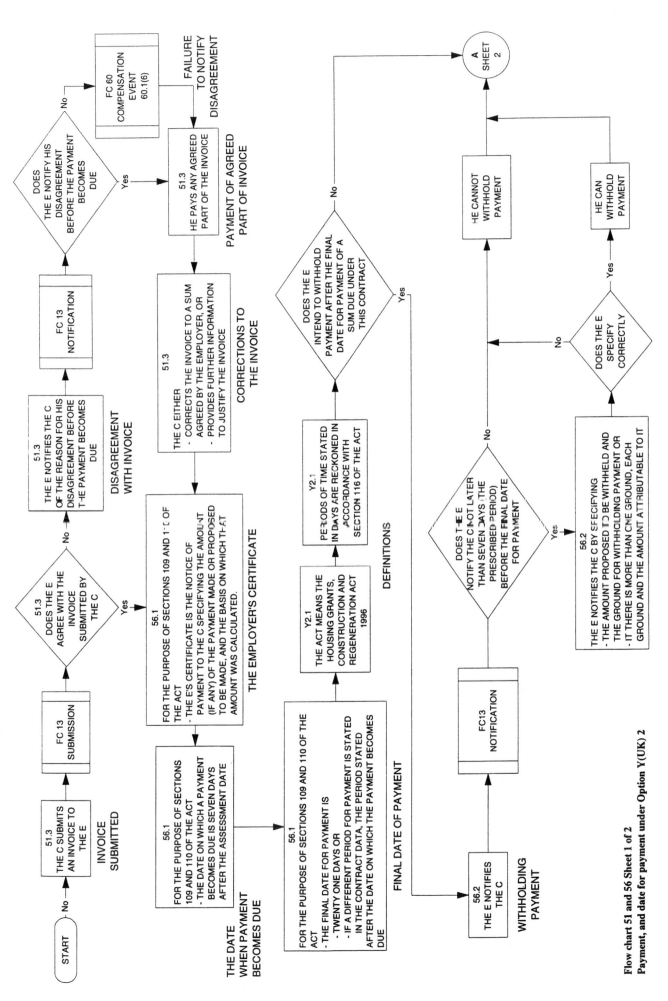

START No

51.3
THE C SUBMITS AN INVOICE TO THE E

INVOICE SUBMITTED

FC 13 SUBMISSION

51.3
DOES THE E AGREE WITH THE INVOICE SUBMITTED BY THE C

Yes / No

51.3
THE E NOTIFIES THE C OF THE REASON FOR HIS DISAGREEMENT BEFORE THE PAYMENT BECOMES DUE

FC 13 NOTIFICATION

DOES THE E NOTIFY HIS DISAGREEMENT BEFORE THE PAYMENT BECOMES DUE

No / Yes

FC 60 COMPENSATION EVENT 60.1(6)

FAILURE TO NOTIFY DISAGREEMENT

DISAGREEMENT WITH INVOICE

51.3
THE C EITHER
- CORRECTS THE INVOICE TO A SUM AGREED BY THE EMPLOYER, OR
- PROVIDES FURTHER INFORMATION TO JUSTIFY THE INVOICE

51.3
HE PAYS ANY AGREED PART OF THE INVOICE

PAYMENT OF AGREED PART OF INVOICE

CORRECTIONS TO THE INVOICE

56.1
FOR THE PURPOSE OF SECTIONS 109 AND 110 OF THE ACT
- THE E'S CERTIFICATE IS THE NOTICE OF PAYMENT TO THE C SPECIFYING THE AMOUNT (IF ANY) OF THE PAYMENT MADE OR PROPOSED TO BE MADE, AND THE BASIS ON WHICH THAT AMOUNT WAS CALCULATED.

THE EMPLOYER'S CERTIFICATE

56.1
FOR THE PURPOSE OF SECTIONS 109 AND 110 OF THE ACT
- THE DATE ON WHICH A PAYMENT BECOMES DUE IS SEVEN DAYS AFTER THE ASSESSMENT DATE

THE DATE WHEN PAYMENT BECOMES DUE

56.1
FOR THE PURPOSE OF SECTIONS 109 AND 110 OF THE ACT
- THE FINAL DATE FOR PAYMENT IS
  - TWENTY ONE DAYS OR
  - IF A DIFFERENT PERIOD FOR PAYMENT IS STATED IN THE CONTRACT DATA, THE PERIOD STATED
AFTER THE DATE ON WHICH THE PAYMENT BECOMES DUE

FINAL DATE OF PAYMENT

Y2.1
THE ACT MEANS THE HOUSING GRANTS, CONSTRUCTION AND REGENERATION ACT 1996

Y2.1
PERIODS OF TIME STATED IN DAYS ARE RECKONED IN ACCORDANCE WITH SECTION 116 OF THE ACT

DEFINITIONS

DOES THE E INTEND TO WITHHOLD PAYMENT AFTER THE FINAL DATE FOR PAYMENT OF A SUM DUE UNDER THIS CONTRACT

No / Yes

DOES THE E NOTIFY THE C NOT LATER THAN SEVEN DAYS (THE PRESCRIBED PERIOD) BEFORE THE FINAL DATE FOR PAYMENT

No / Yes

FC13 NOTIFICATION

56.2
THE E NOTIFIES THE C

WITHHOLDING PAYMENT

56.2
THE E NOTIFIES THE C BY SPECIFYING
- THE AMOUNT PROPOSED TO BE WITHHELD AND THE GROUND FOR WITHHOLDING PAYMENT OR
- IF THERE IS MORE THAN ONE GROUND, EACH GROUND AND THE AMOUNT ATTRIBUTABLE TO IT

DOES THE E SPECIFY CORRECTLY

Yes / No

HE CANNOT WITHHOLD PAYMENT

HE CAN WITHHOLD PAYMENT

A SHEET 2

Flow chart 51 and 56 Sheet 1 of 2
Payment, and date for payment under Option Y(UK) 2

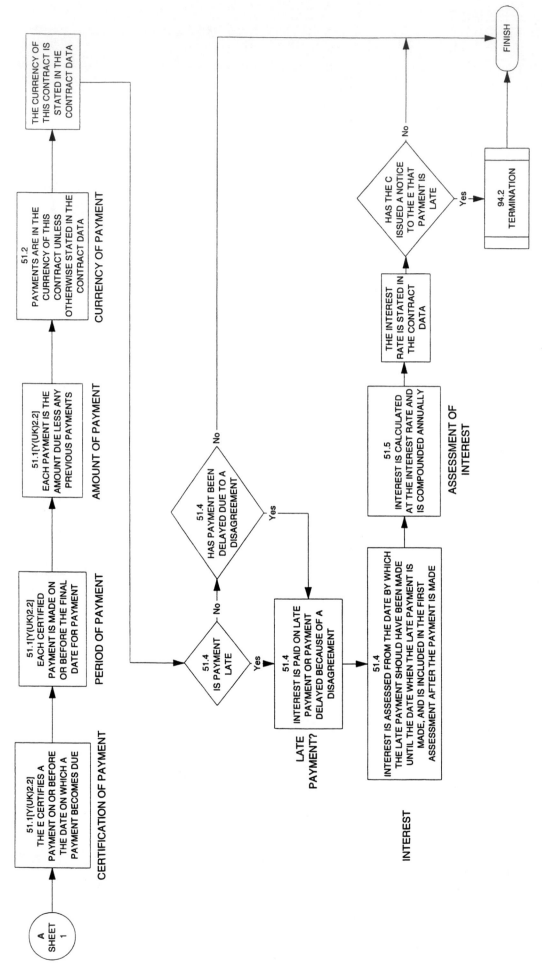

CERTIFICATION OF PAYMENT

51.1[Y(UK)2.2]
THE E CERTIFIES A PAYMENT ON OR BEFORE THE DATE ON WHICH A PAYMENT BECOMES DUE

PERIOD OF PAYMENT

51.1[Y(UK)2.2]
EACH CERTIFIED PAYMENT IS MADE ON OR BEFORE THE FINAL DATE FOR PAYMENT

AMOUNT OF PAYMENT

51.1[Y(UK)2.2]
EACH PAYMENT IS THE AMOUNT DUE LESS ANY PREVIOUS PAYMENTS

CURRENCY OF PAYMENT

51.2
PAYMENTS ARE IN THE CURRENCY OF THIS CONTRACT UNLESS OTHERWISE STATED IN THE CONTRACT DATA

THE CURRENCY OF THIS CONTRACT IS STATED IN THE CONTRACT DATA

LATE PAYMENT?

51.4
IS PAYMENT LATE

51.4
HAS PAYMENT BEEN DELAYED DUE TO A DISAGREEMENT

INTEREST

51.4
INTEREST IS PAID ON LATE PAYMENT OR PAYMENT DELAYED BECAUSE OF A DISAGREEMENT

51.4
INTEREST IS ASSESSED FROM THE DATE BY WHICH THE LATE PAYMENT SHOULD HAVE BEEN MADE UNTIL THE DATE WHEN THE LATE PAYMENT IS MADE, AND IS INCLUDED IN THE FIRST ASSESSMENT AFTER THE PAYMENT IS MADE

ASSESSMENT OF INTEREST

51.5
INTEREST IS CALCULATED AT THE INTEREST RATE AND IS COMPOUNDED ANNUALLY

THE INTEREST RATE IS STATED IN THE CONTRACT DATA

HAS THE C ISSUED A NOTICE TO THE E THAT PAYMENT IS LATE

94.2
TERMINATION

FINISH

A SHEET 1

70

Flow chart 51 and 56 Sheet 2 of 2
Payment, and date for payment under Option Y(UK) 2

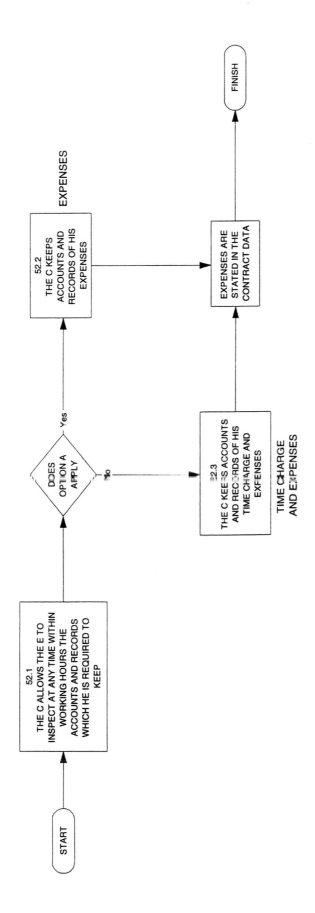

START

52.1
THE C ALLOWS THE E TO
INSPECT AT ANY TIME WITHIN
WORKING HOURS THE
ACCOUNTS AND RECORDS
WHICH HE IS REQUIRED TO
KEEP

DOES
OPTION A
APPLY

Yes

No

52.2
THE C KEEPS
ACCOUNTS AND
RECORDS OF HIS
EXPENSES

EXPENSES

52.3
THE C KEEPS ACCOUNTS
AND RECORDS OF HIS
TIME CHARGE AND
EXPENSES

TIME CHARGE
AND EXPENSES

EXPENSES ARE
STATED IN THE
CONTRACT DATA

FINISH

Flow chart 52
Accounts and Records

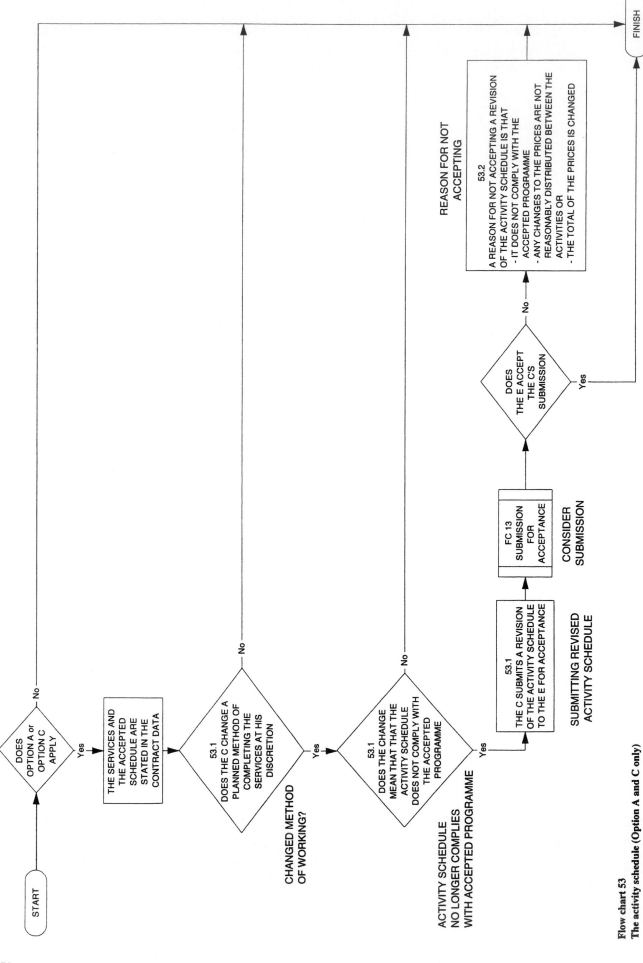

Flow chart 53

The activity schedule (Option A and C only)

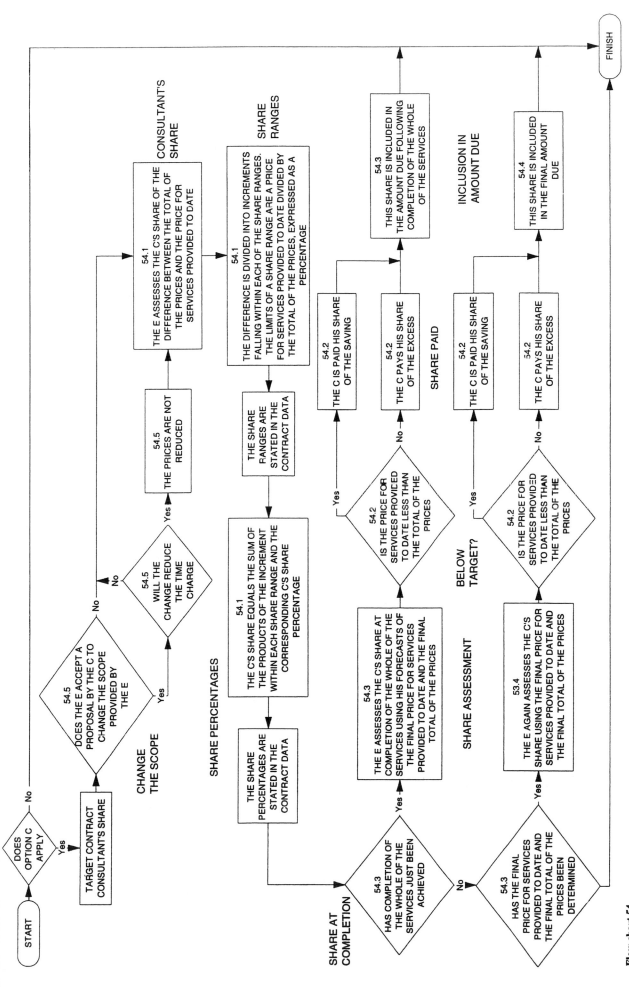

Flow chart 54
The Consultant's share (used only with Option C)

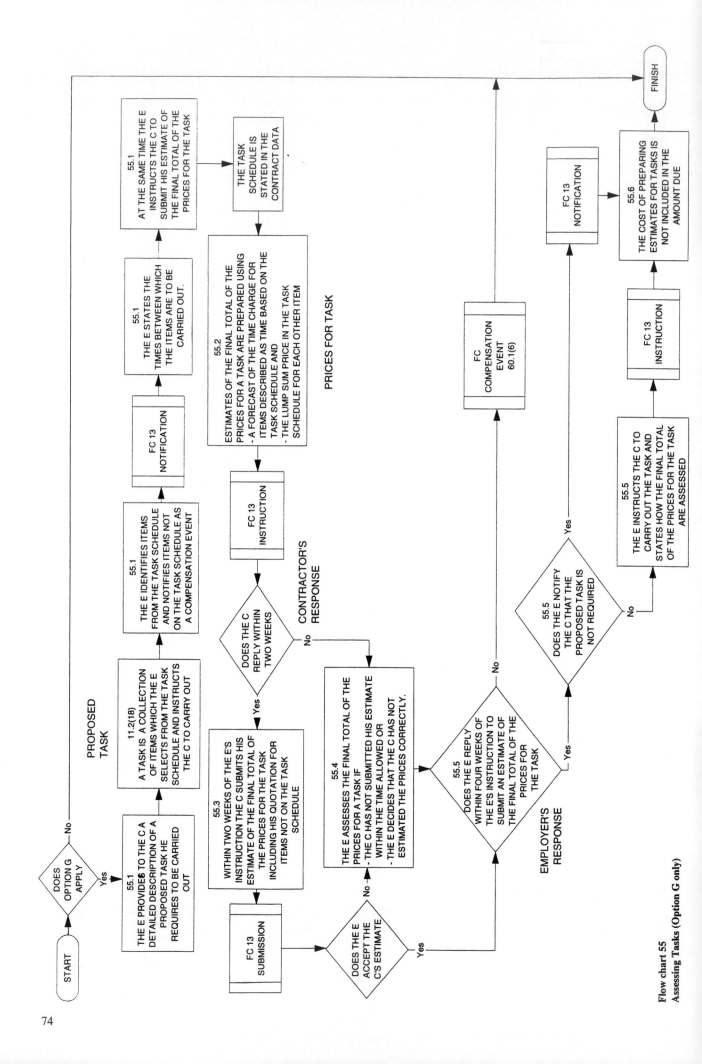

Flow chart 55
Assessing Tasks (Option G only)

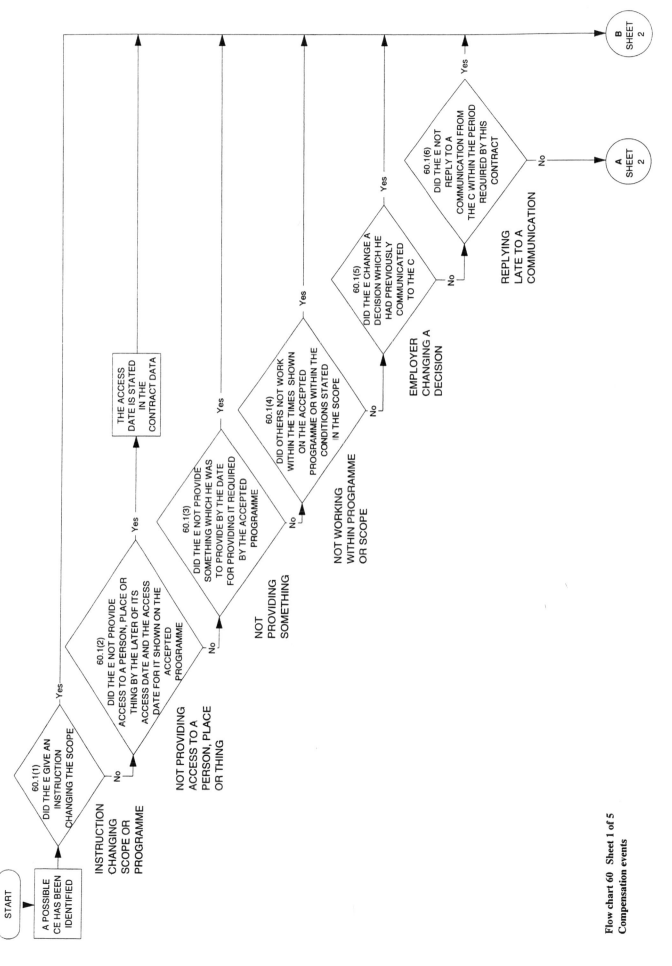

START

A POSSIBLE
CE HAS BEEN
IDENTIFIED

60.1(1)
DID THE E GIVE AN
INSTRUCTION
CHANGING THE SCOPE

INSTRUCTION
CHANGING
SCOPE OR
PROGRAMME

Yes

No

60.1(2)
DID THE E NOT PROVIDE
ACCESS TO A PERSON, PLACE OR
THING BY THE LATER OF ITS
ACCESS DATE AND THE ACCESS
DATE FOR IT SHOWN ON THE
ACCEPTED
PROGRAMME

NOT PROVIDING
ACCESS TO A
PERSON, PLACE
OR THING

Yes

THE ACCESS
DATE IS STATED
IN THE
CONTRACT DATA

No

60.1(3)
DID THE E NOT PROVIDE
SOMETHING WHICH HE WAS
TO PROVIDE BY THE DATE
FOR PROVIDING IT REQUIRED
BY THE ACCEPTED
PROGRAMME

NOT
PROVIDING
SOMETHING

Yes

No

60.1(4)
DID OTHERS NOT WORK
WITHIN THE TIMES SHOWN
ON THE ACCEPTED
PROGRAMME OR WITHIN THE
CONDITIONS STATED
IN THE SCOPE

NOT WORKING
WITHIN PROGRAMME
OR SCOPE

Yes

No

60.1(5)
DID THE E CHANGE A
DECISION WHICH HE
HAD PREVIOUSLY
COMMUNICATED
TO THE C

EMPLOYER
CHANGING A
DECISION

Yes

No

60.1(6)
DID THE E NOT
REPLY TO A
COMMUNICATION FROM
THE C WITHIN THE PERIOD
REQUIRED BY THIS
CONTRACT

REPLYING
LATE TO A
COMMUNICATION

Yes

No

B
SHEET
2

A
SHEET
2

Flow chart 60   Sheet 1 of 5
Compensation events

75

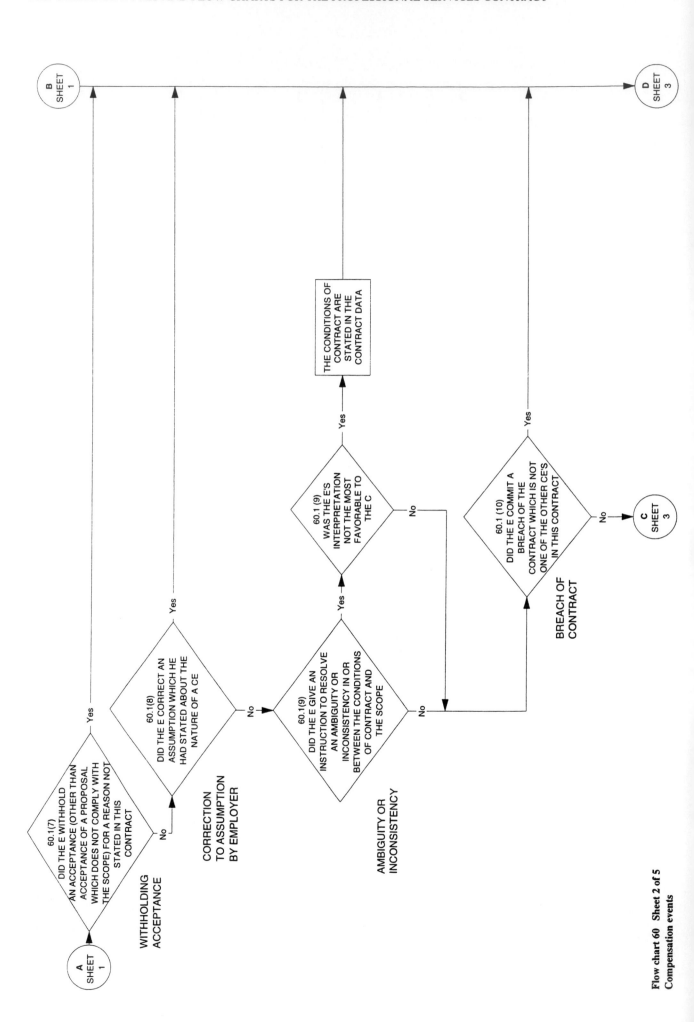

Flow chart 60   Sheet 2 of 5
Compensation events

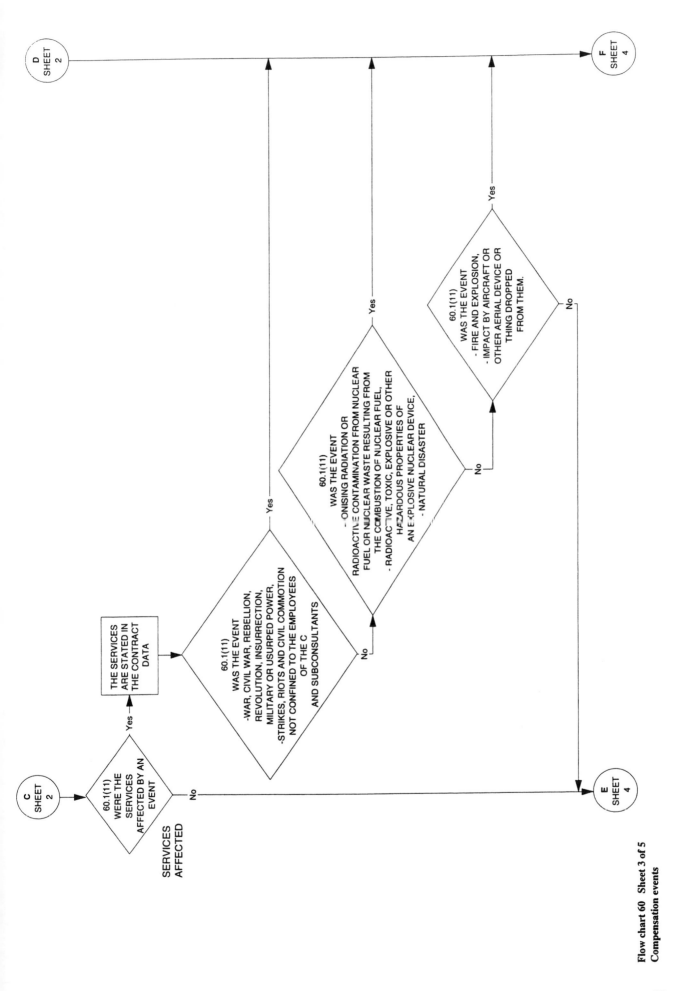

Flow chart 60 Sheet 3 of 5
Compensation events

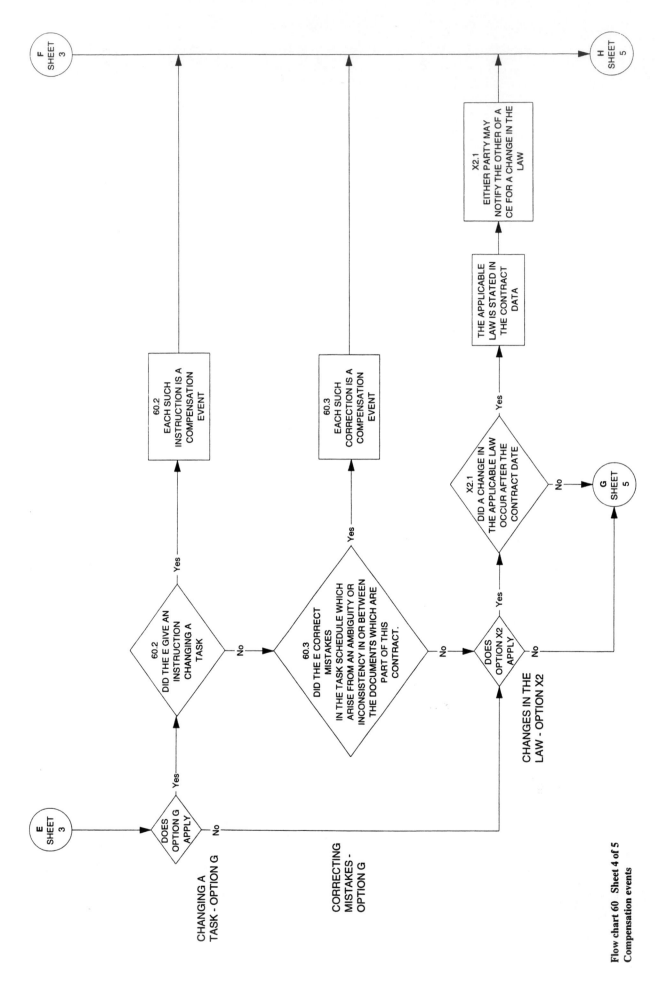

Flow chart 60   Sheet 4 of 5
Compensation events

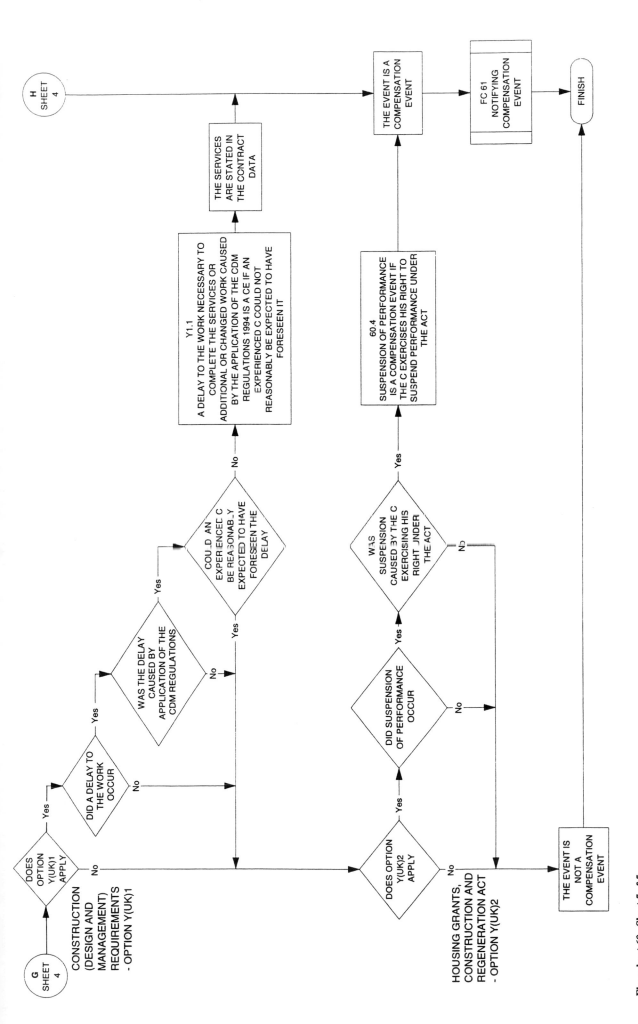

Flow chart 60   Sheet 5 of 5
Compensation events

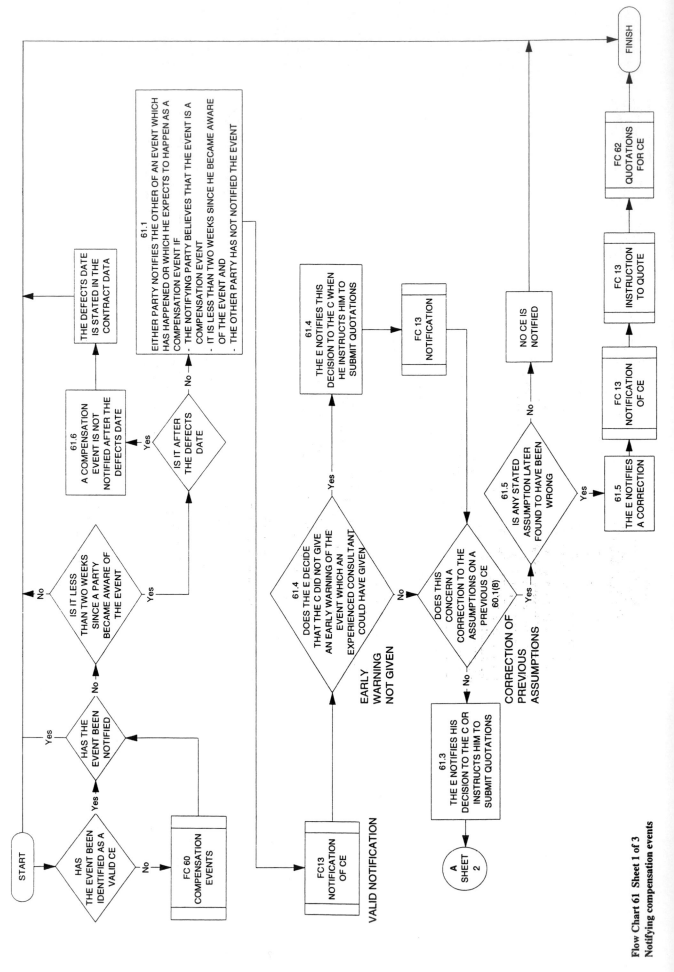

Flow Chart 61 Sheet 1 of 3
Notifying compensation events

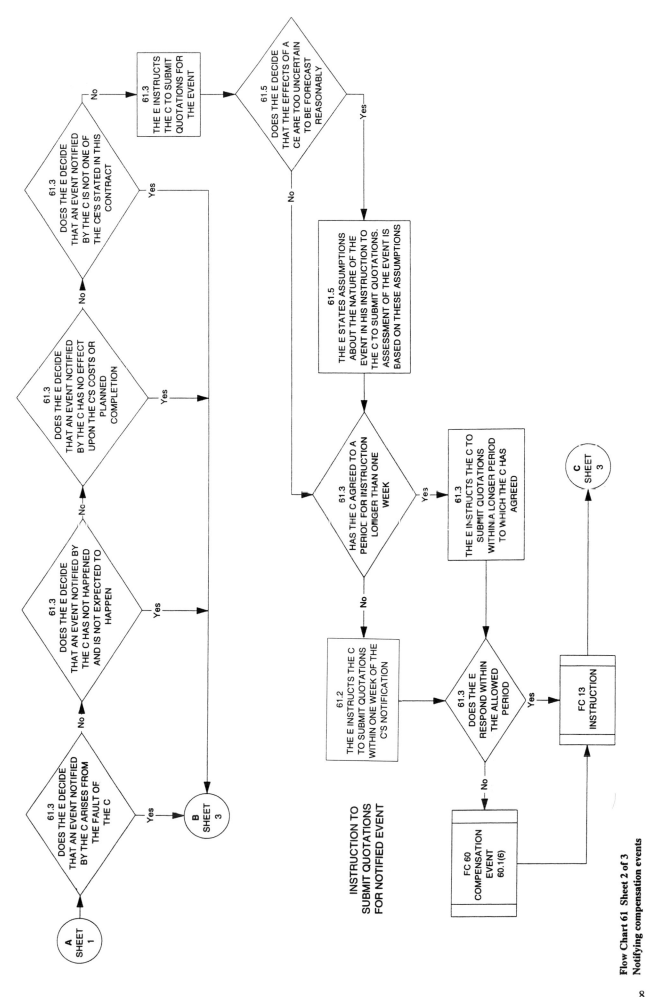

Flow Chart 61 Sheet 2 of 3
Notifying compensation events

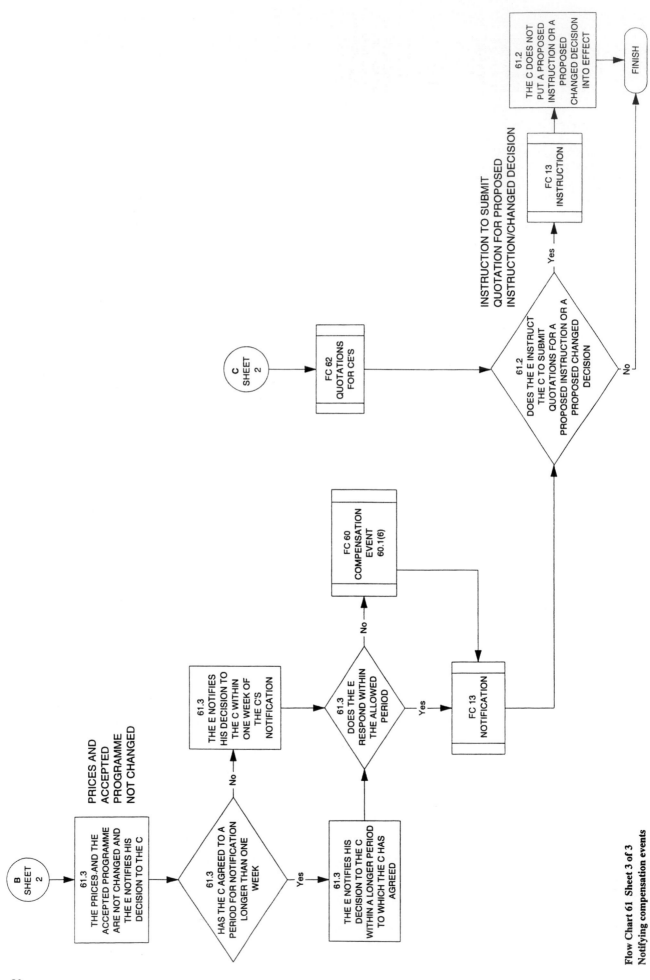

Flow Chart 61 Sheet 3 of 3
Notifying compensation events

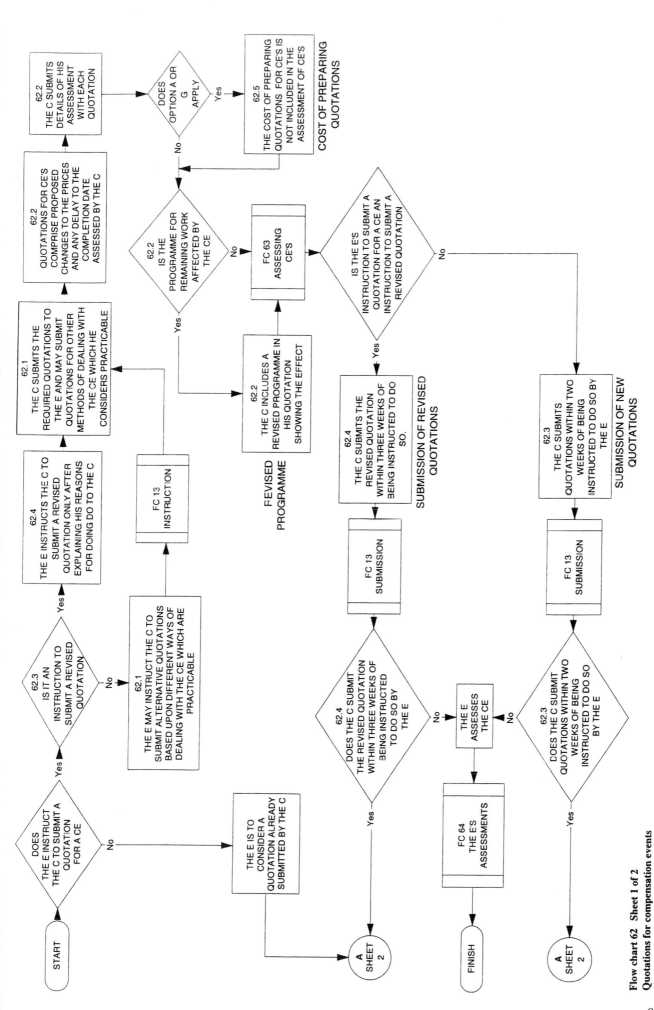

Flow chart 62 Sheet 1 of 2
Quotations for compensation events

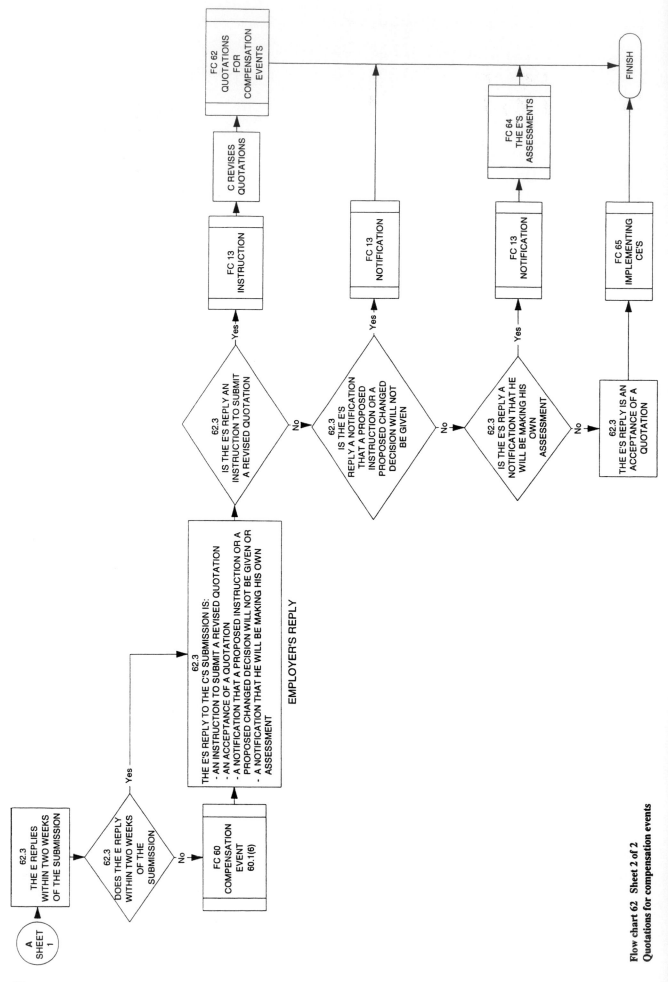

Flow chart 62   Sheet 2 of 2
Quotations for compensation events

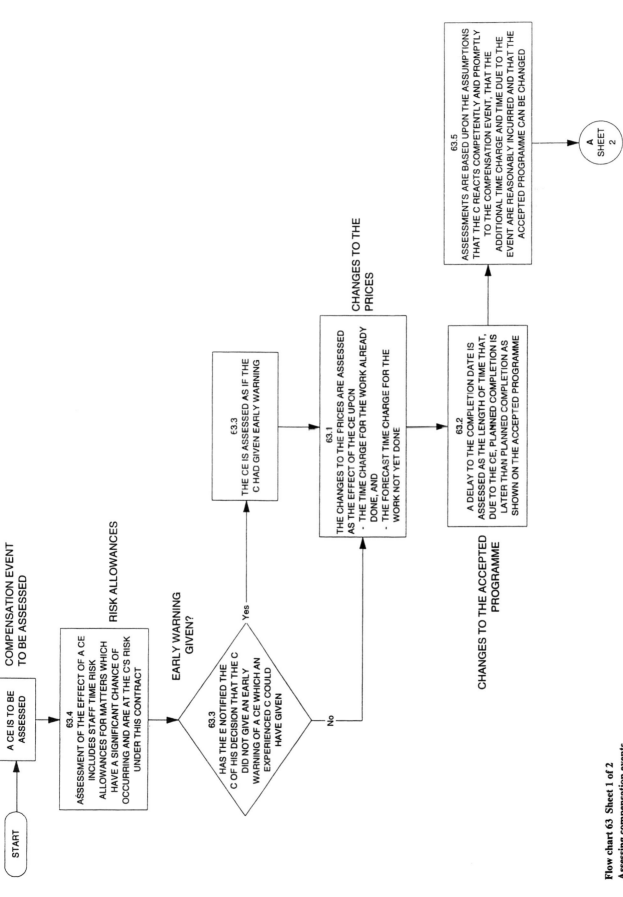

Flow chart 63 Sheet 1 of 2
Assessing compensation events

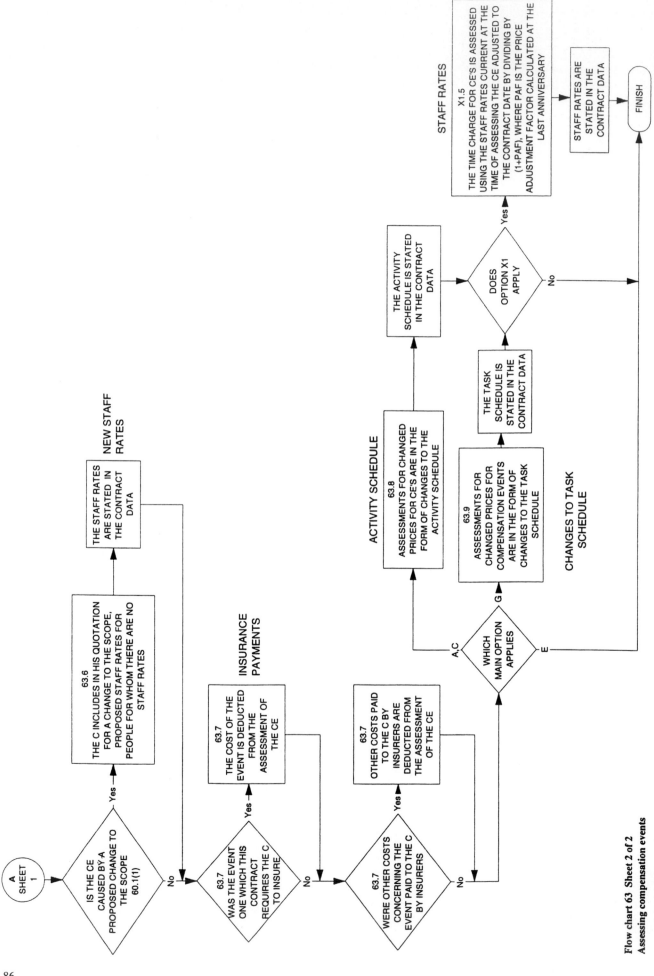

Flow chart 63 Sheet 2 of 2
Assessing compensation events

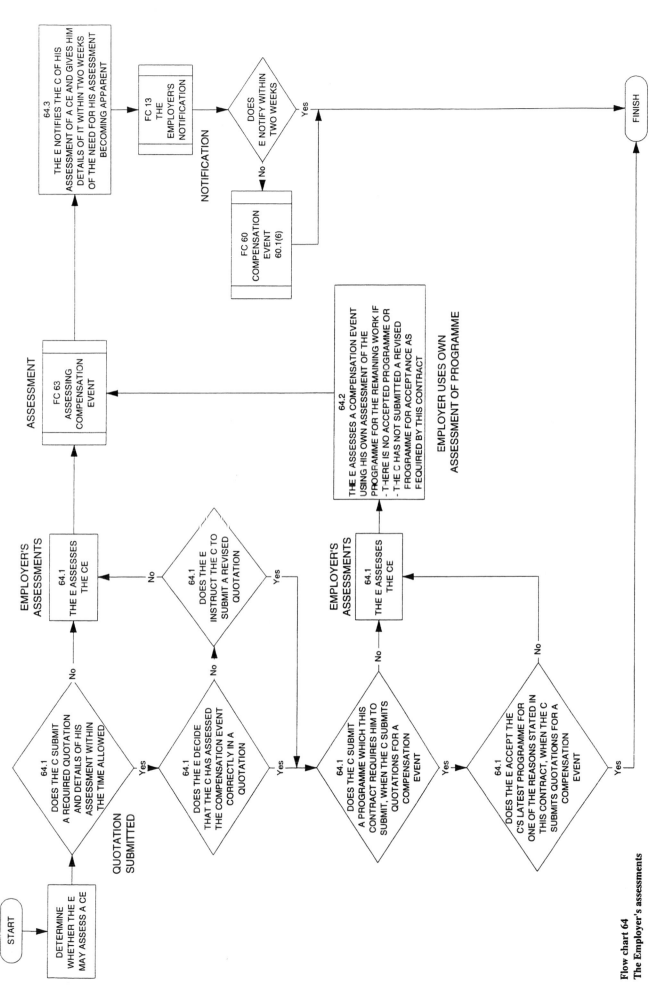

Flow chart 64
The Employer's assessments

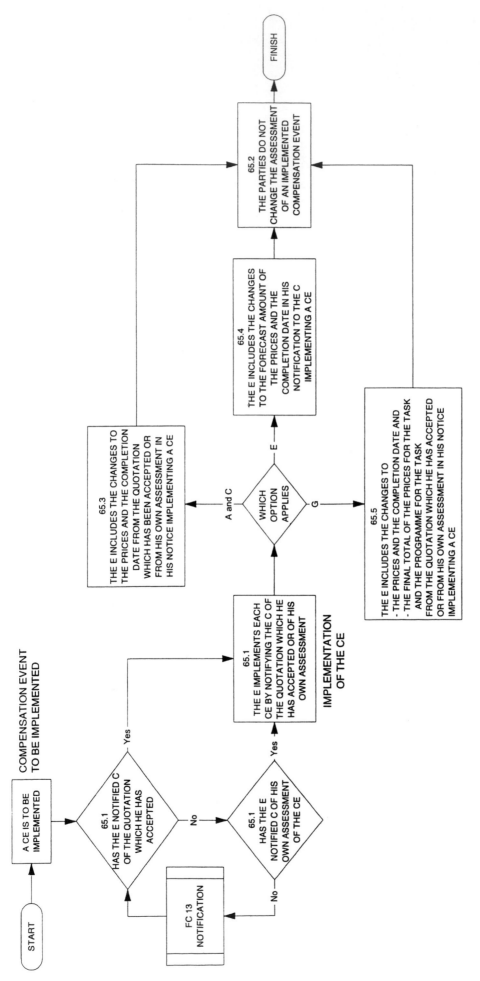

Flow chart 65
Implementing compensation events

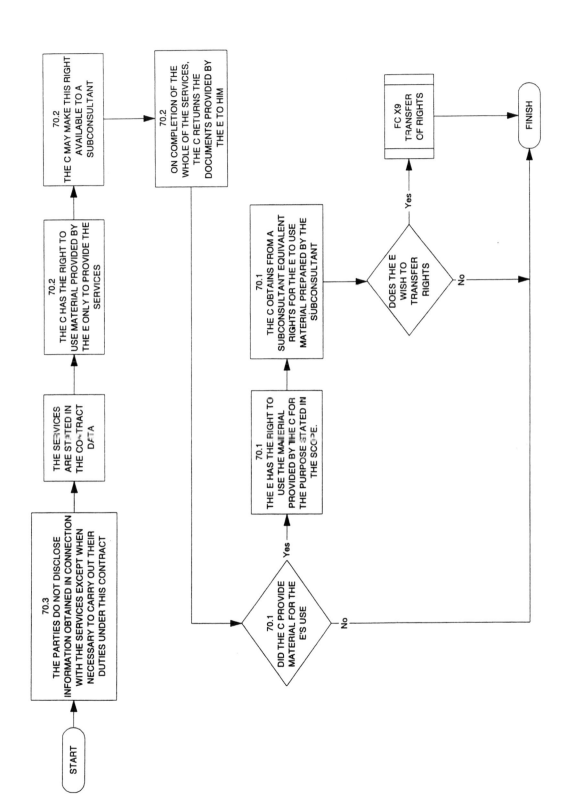

Flow chart 70
The Parties' use of material

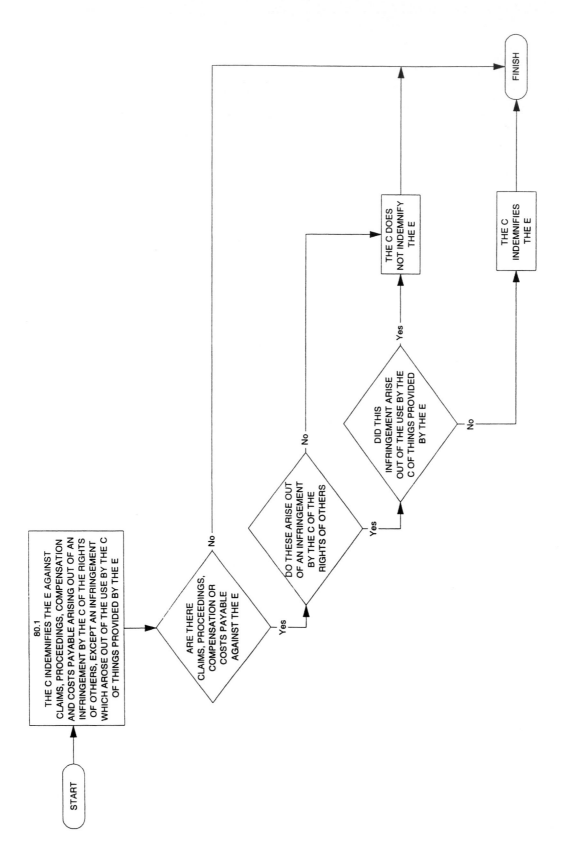

Flow chart 80
Indemnity

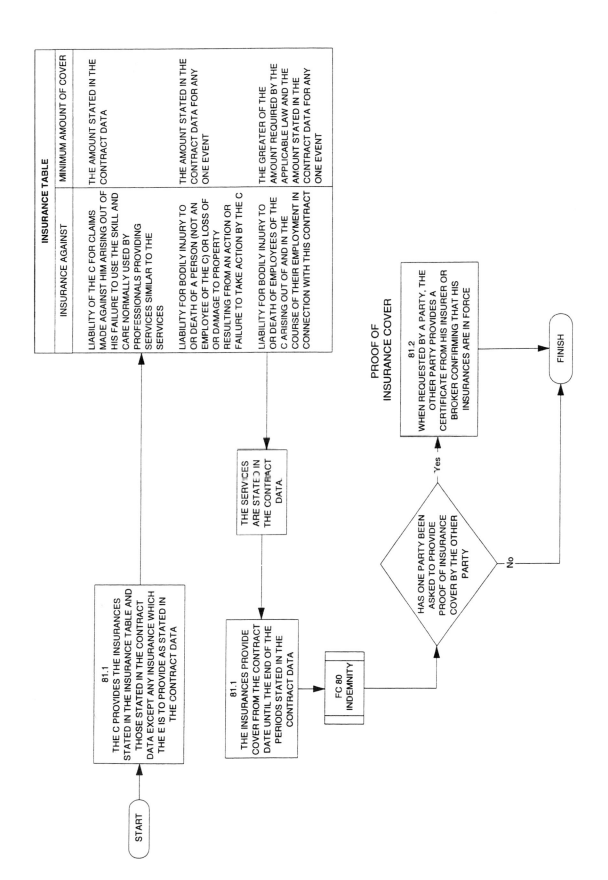

INSURANCE TABLE

INSURANCE AGAINST	MINIMUM AMOUNT OF COVER
LIABILITY OF THE C FOR CLAIMS MADE AGAINST HIM ARISING OUT OF HIS FAILURE TO USE THE SKILL AND CARE NORMALLY USED BY PROFESSIONALS PROVIDING SERVICES SIMILAR TO THE SERVICES	THE AMOUNT STATED IN THE CONTRACT DATA
LIABILITY FOR BODILY INJURY TO OR DEATH OF A PERSON (NOT AN EMPLOYEE OF THE C) OR LOSS OF OR DAMAGE TO PROPERTY RESULTING FROM AN ACTION OR FAILURE TO TAKE ACTION BY THE C	THE AMOUNT STATED IN THE CONTRACT DATA FOR ANY ONE EVENT
LIABILITY FOR BODILY INJURY TO OR DEATH OF EMPLOYEES OF THE C ARISING OUT OF AND IN THE COURSE OF THEIR EMPLOYMENT IN CONNECTION WITH THIS CONTRACT	THE GREATER OF THE AMOUNT REQUIRED BY THE APPLICABLE LAW AND THE AMOUNT STATED IN THE CONTRACT DATA FOR ANY ONE EVENT

START

81.1
THE C PROVIDES THE INSURANCES STATED IN THE INSURANCE TABLE AND THOSE STATED IN THE CONTRACT DATA EXCEPT ANY INSURANCE WHICH THE E IS TO PROVIDE AS STATED IN THE CONTRACT DATA

THE SERVICES ARE STATED IN THE CONTRACT DATA.

81.1
THE INSURANCES PROVIDE COVER FROM THE CONTRACT DATE UNTIL THE END OF THE PERIODS STATED IN THE CONTRACT DATA

FC 80
INDEMNITY

PROOF OF
INSURANCE COVER

HAS ONE PARTY BEEN ASKED TO PROVIDE PROOF OF INSURANCE COVER BY THE OTHER PARTY

Yes

No

81.2
WHEN REQUESTED BY A PARTY, THE OTHER PARTY PROVIDES A CERTIFICATE FROM HIS INSURER OR BROKER CONFIRMING THAT HIS INSURANCES ARE IN FORCE

FINISH

Flow chart 81
Insurance cover

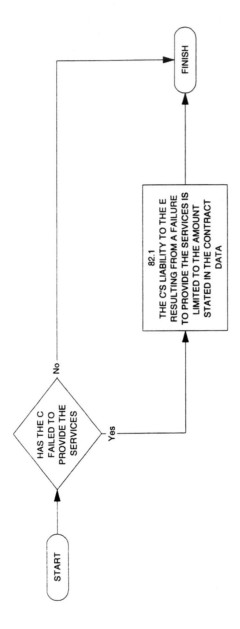

Flow chart 82
Limit on the *Consultant*'s liability

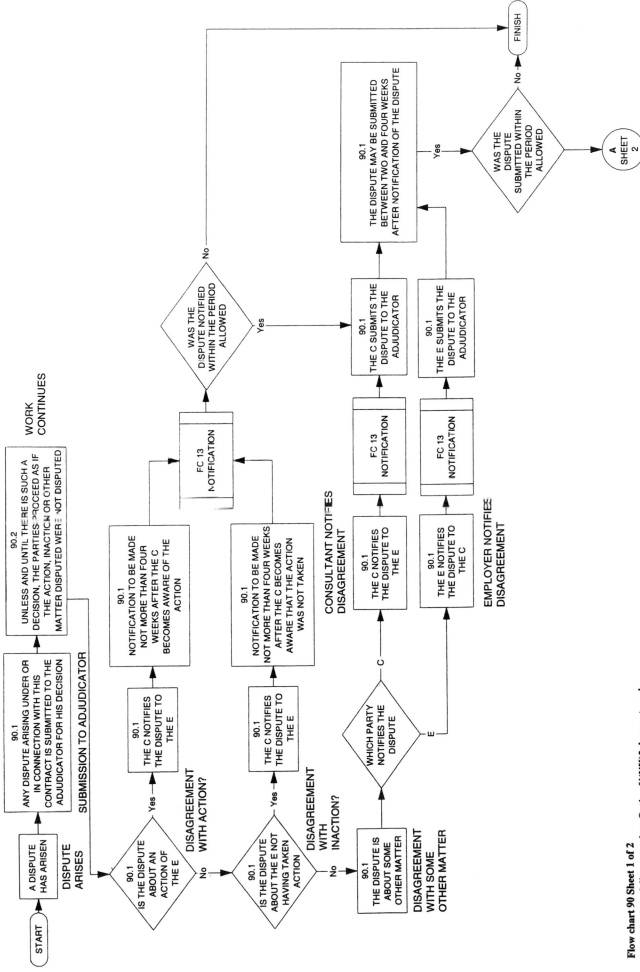

Flow chart 90 Sheet 1 of 2
Adjudication of disputes when Option Y(UK)2 does not apply

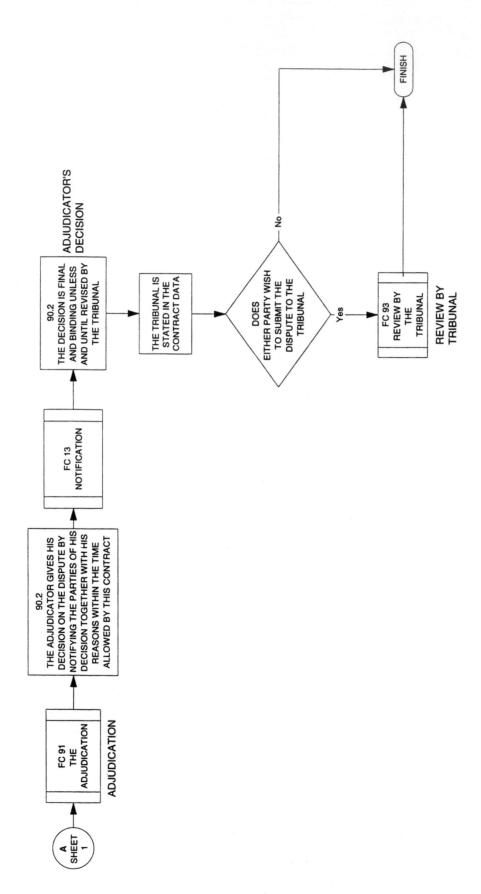

Flow chart 90 Sheet 2 of 2
Adjudication of disputes when Option Y(UK)2 does not apply

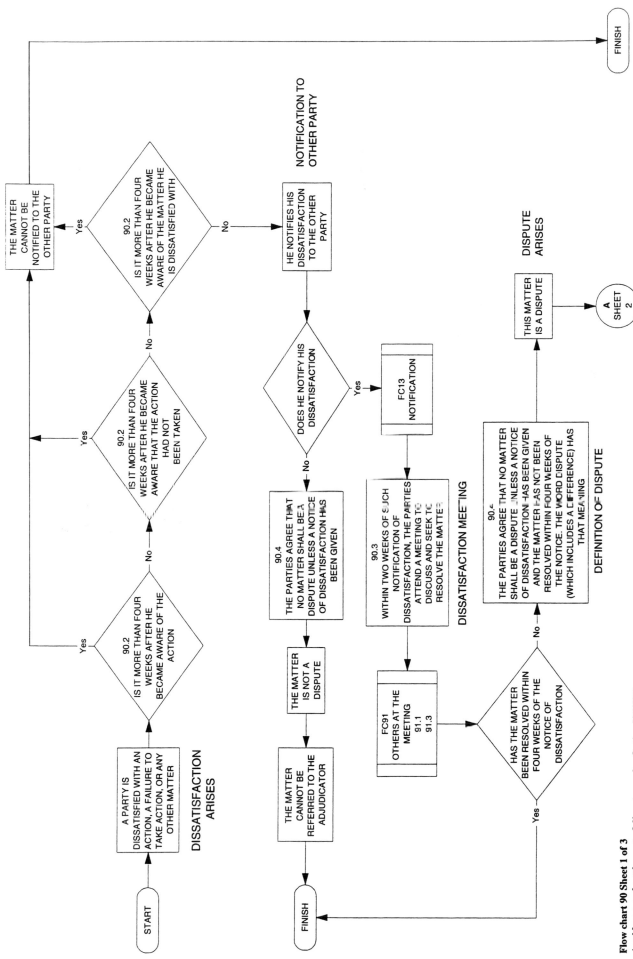

Flow chart 90 Sheet 1 of 3
Avoidance and settlement of disputes under Option Y(UK)2

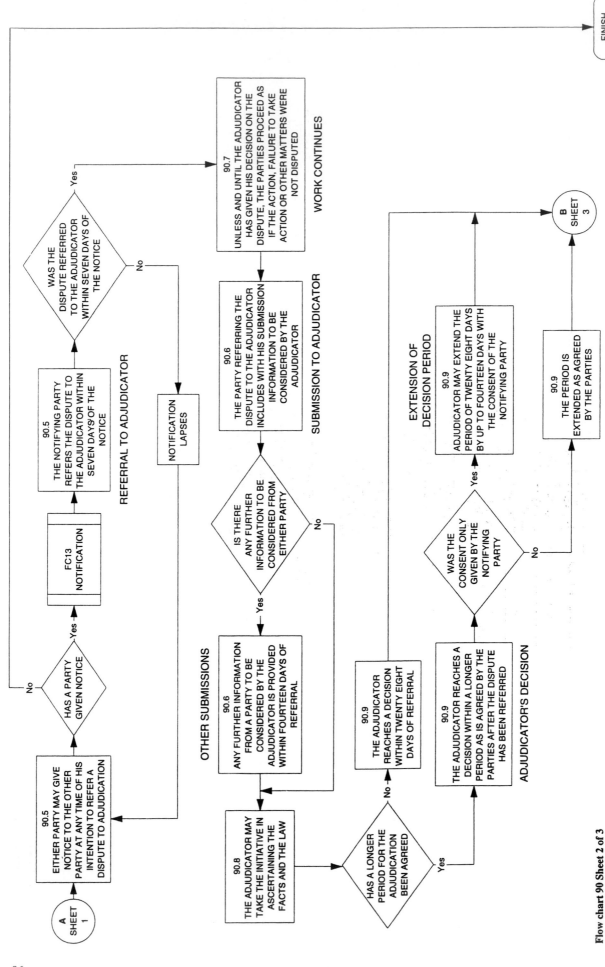

Flow chart 90 Sheet 2 of 3
Avoidance and settlement of disputes under Option Y(UK)2

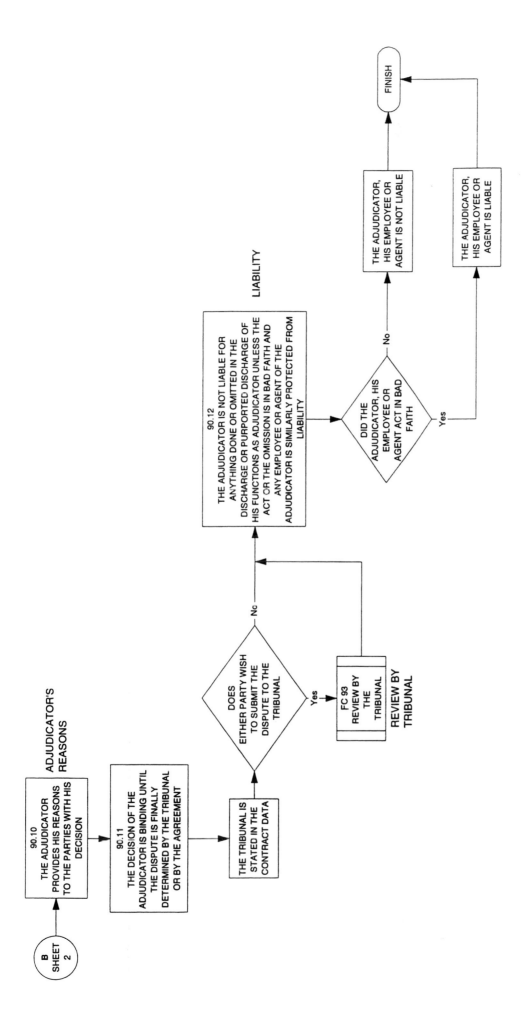

Flow chart 90 Sheet 3 of 3
Avoidance and settlement of disputes under Option Y(UK)2

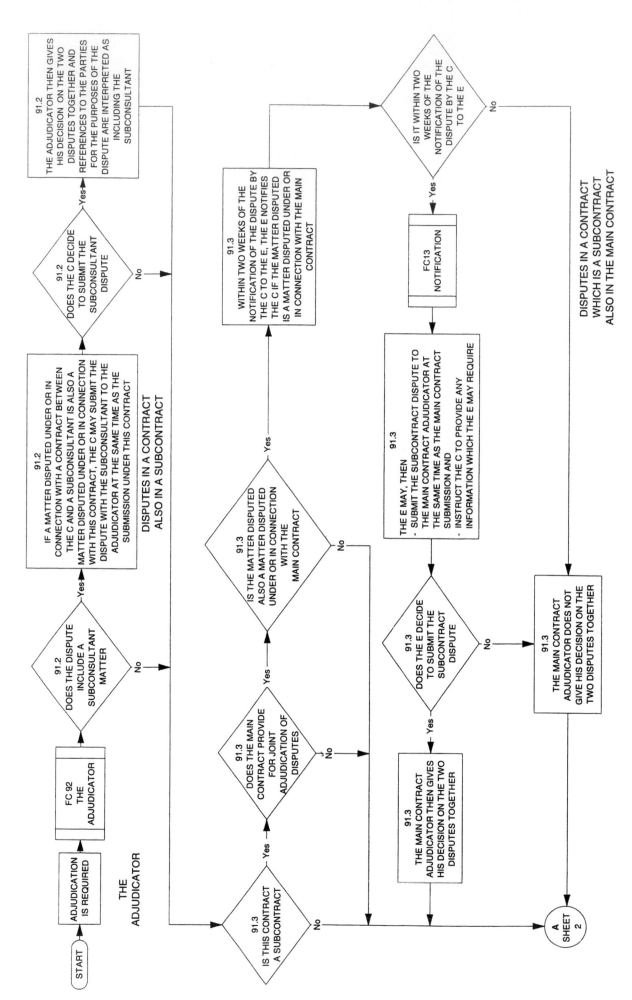

Flow chart 91 Sheet 1 of 3
The adjudication when Option Y(UK)2 does not apply

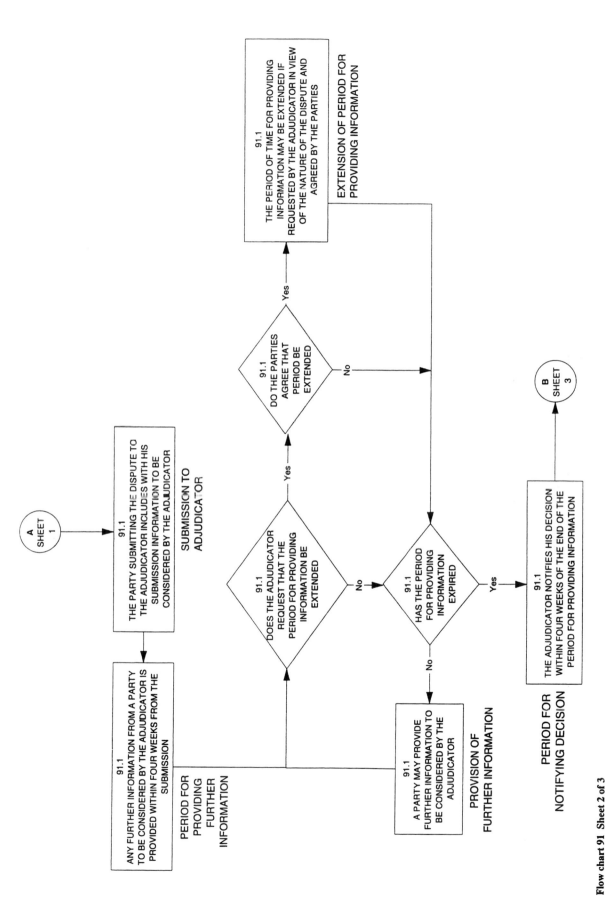

A
SHEET
1

91.1
THE PARTY SUBMITTING THE DISPUTE TO THE ADJUDICATOR INCLUDES WITH HIS SUBMISSION INFORMATION TO BE CONSIDERED BY THE ADJUDICATOR

SUBMISSION TO ADJUDICATOR

91.1
ANY FURTHER INFORMATION FROM A PARTY TO BE CONSIDERED BY THE ADJUDICATOR IS PROVIDED WITHIN FOUR WEEKS FROM THE SUBMISSION

PERIOD FOR PROVIDING FURTHER INFORMATION

91.1
DOES THE ADJUDICATOR REQUEST THAT THE PERIOD FOR PROVIDING INFORMATION BE EXTENDED

Yes

No

91.1
DO THE PARTIES AGREE THAT PERIOD BE EXTENDED

Yes

No

91.1
THE PERIOD OF TIME FOR PROVIDING INFORMATION MAY BE EXTENDED IF REQUESTED BY THE ADJUDICATOR IN VIEW OF THE NATURE OF THE DISPUTE AND AGREED BY THE PARTIES

EXTENSION OF PERIOD FOR PROVIDING INFORMATION

91.1
HAS THE PERIOD FOR PROVIDING INFORMATION EXPIRED

Yes

No

91.1
A PARTY MAY PROVIDE FURTHER INFORMATION TO BE CONSIDERED BY THE ADJUDICATOR

PROVISION OF FURTHER INFORMATION

91.1
THE ADJUDICATOR NOTIFIES HIS DECISION WITHIN FOUR WEEKS OF THE END OF THE PERIOD FOR PROVIDING INFORMATION

PERIOD FOR NOTIFYING DECISION

B
SHEET
3

Flow chart 91 Sheet 2 of 3
The adjudication when Option Y(UK)2 does not apply

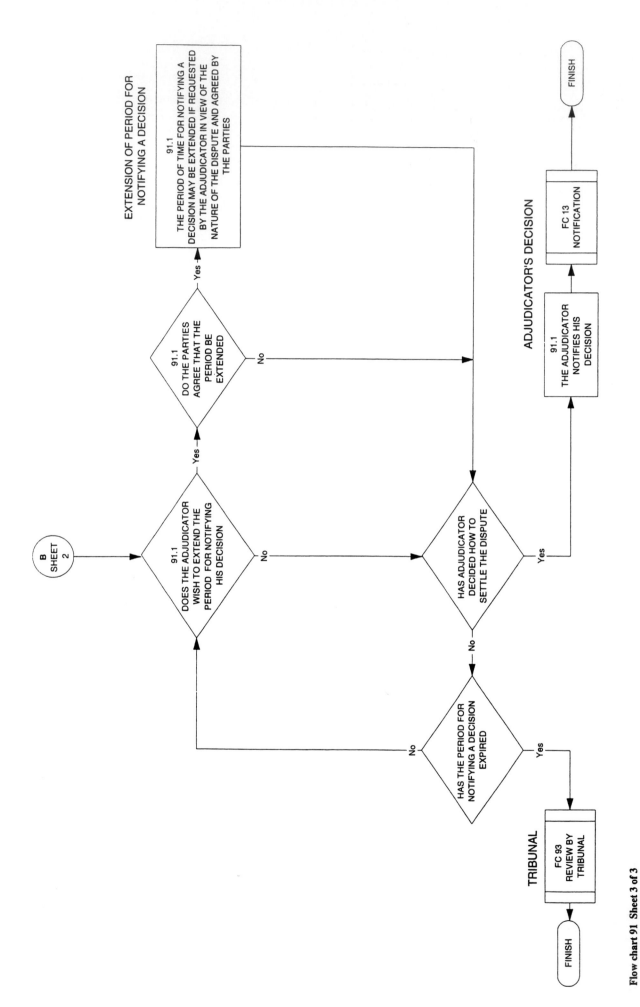

EXTENSION OF PERIOD FOR
NOTIFYING A DECISION

91.1
THE PERIOD OF TIME FOR NOTIFYING A
DECISION MAY BE EXTENDED IF REQUESTED
BY THE ADJUDICATOR IN VIEW OF THE
NATURE OF THE DISPUTE AND AGREED BY
THE PARTIES

91.1
DO THE PARTIES
AGREE THAT THE
PERIOD BE
EXTENDED

Yes

No

B
SHEET
2

91.1
DOES THE ADJUDICATOR
WISH TO EXTEND THE
PERIOD FOR NOTIFYING
HIS DECISION

Yes

No

HAS ADJUDICATOR
DECIDED HOW TO
SETTLE THE DISPUTE

Yes

No

HAS THE PERIOD FOR
NOTIFYING A DECISION
EXPIRED

No

Yes

ADJUDICATOR'S DECISION

91.1
THE ADJUDICATOR
NOTIFIES HIS
DECISION

FC 13
NOTIFICATION

FINISH

TRIBUNAL

FC 93
REVIEW BY
TRIBUNAL

FINISH

Flow chart 91 Sheet 3 of 3
The adjudication when Option Y(UK)2 does not apply

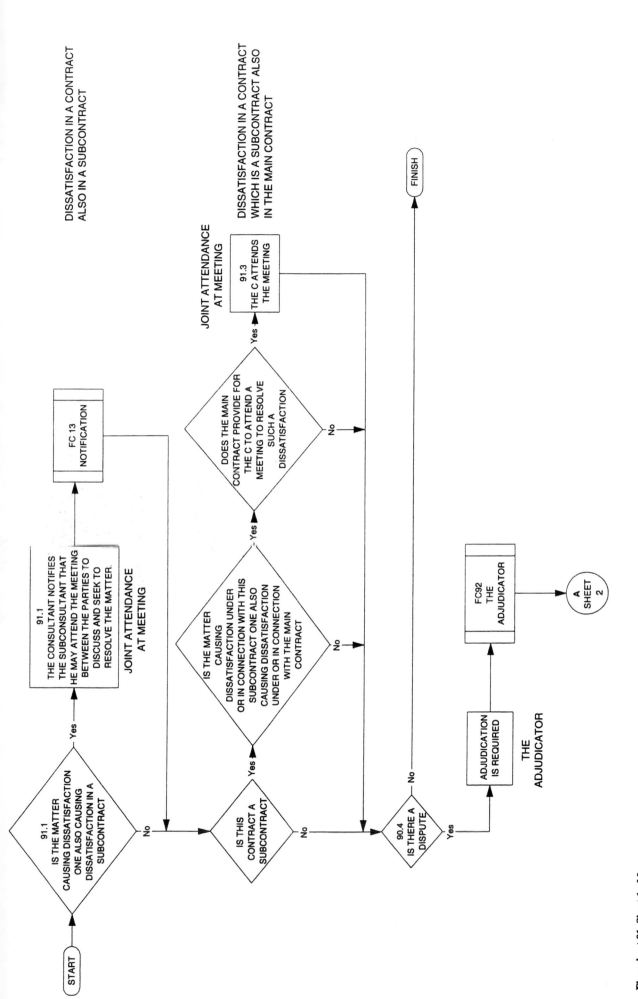

DISSATISFACTION IN A CONTRACT ALSO IN A SUBCONTRACT

DISSATISFACTION IN A CONTRACT WHICH IS A SUBCONTRACT ALSO IN THE MAIN CONTRACT

JOINT ATTENDANCE AT MEETING

91.3
THE C ATTENDS THE MEETING

FC 13
NOTIFICATION

91.1
THE CONSULTANT NOTIFIES THE SUBCONSULTANT THAT HE MAY ATTEND THE MEETING BETWEEN THE PARTIES TO DISCUSS AND SEEK TO RESOLVE THE MATTER.

JOINT ATTENDANCE AT MEETING

DOES THE MAIN CONTRACT PROVIDE FOR THE C TO ATTEND A MEETING TO RESOLVE SUCH A DISSATISFACTION

Yes

No

IS THE MATTER CAUSING DISSATISFACTION UNDER OR IN CONNECTION WITH THIS SUBCONTRACT ONE ALSO CAUSING DISSATISFACTION UNDER OR IN CONNECTION WITH THE MAIN CONTRACT

Yes

No

FINISH

START

91.1
IS THE MATTER CAUSING DISSATISFACTION ONE ALSO CAUSING DISSATISFACTION IN A SUBCONTRACT

Yes

No

IS THIS CONTRACT A SUBCONTRACT

Yes

No

90.4
IS THERE A DISPUTE

No

Yes

ADJUDICATION IS REQUIRED

FC92
THE ADJUDICATOR

THE ADJUDICATOR

A
SHEET
2

Flow chart 91 Sheet 1 of 2
Combining adjudications under Option Y(UK)2

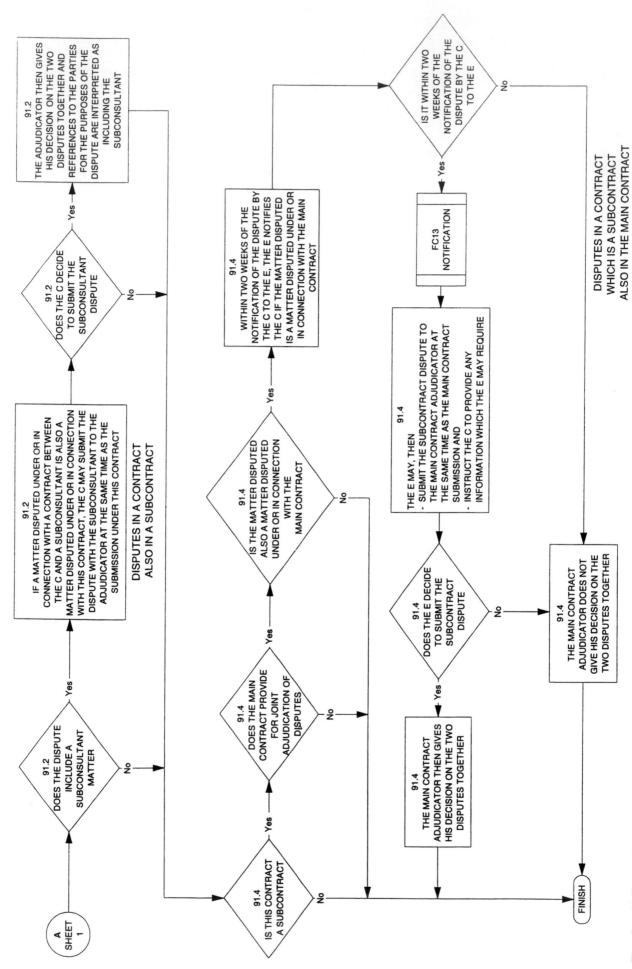

Flow chart 91 Sheet 2 of 2
Combining adjudications under Option Y(UK)2

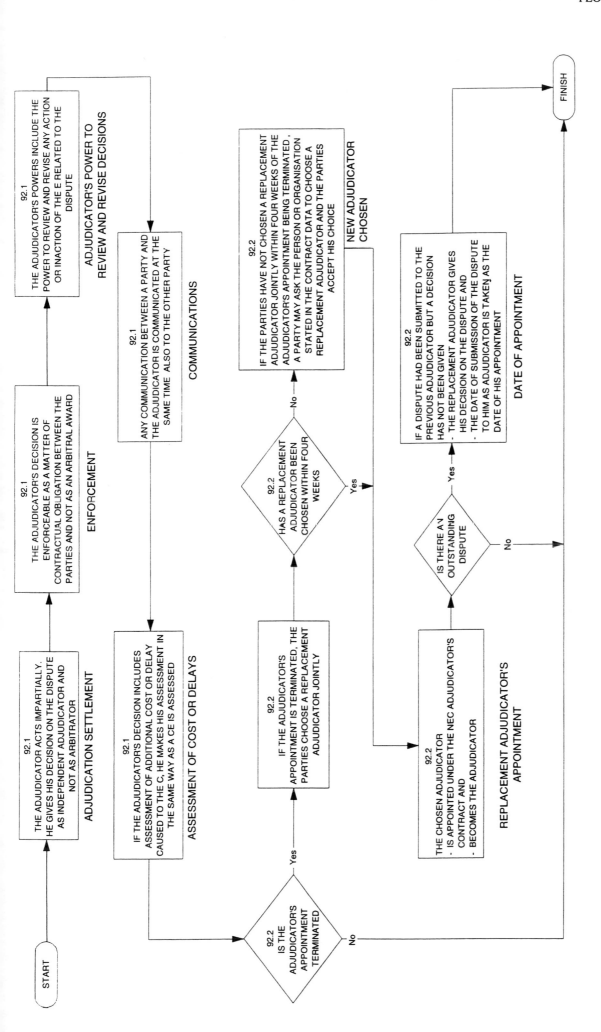

START

92.1
THE ADJUDICATOR ACTS IMPARTIALLY.
HE GIVES HIS DECISION ON THE DISPUTE
AS INDEPENDENT ADJUDICATOR AND
NOT AS ARBITRATOR

ADJUDICATION SETTLEMENT

92.1
THE ADJUDICATOR'S DECISION IS
ENFORCEABLE AS A MATTER OF
CONTRACTUAL OBLIGATION BETWEEN THE
PARTIES AND NOT AS AN ARBITRAL AWARD

ENFORCEMENT

92.1
THE ADJUDICATOR'S POWERS INCLUDE THE
POWER TO REVIEW AND REVISE ANY ACTION
OR INACTION OF THE E RELATED TO THE
DISPUTE

ADJUDICATOR'S POWER TO
REVIEW AND REVISE DECISIONS

92.1
ANY COMMUNICATION BETWEEN A PARTY AND
THE ADJUDICATOR IS COMMUNICATED AT THE
SAME TIME ALSO TO THE OTHER PARTY

COMMUNICATIONS

92.1
IF THE ADJUDICATOR'S DECISION INCLUDES
ASSESSMENT OF ADDITIONAL COST OR DELAY
CAUSED TO THE C, HE MAKES HIS ASSESSMENT IN
THE SAME WAY AS A CE IS ASSESSED

ASSESSMENT OF COST OR DELAYS

92.2
IS THE
ADJUDICATOR'S
APPOINTMENT
TERMINATED

No

Yes

92.2
IF THE ADJUDICATOR'S
APPOINTMENT IS TERMINATED, THE
PARTIES CHOOSE A REPLACEMENT
ADJUDICATOR JOINTLY

92.2
HAS A REPLACEMENT
ADJUDICATOR BEEN
CHOSEN WITHIN FOUR
WEEKS

No

Yes

92.2
IF THE PARTIES HAVE NOT CHOSEN A REPLACEMENT
ADJUDICATOR JOINTLY WITHIN FOUR WEEKS OF THE
ADJUDICATOR'S APPOINTMENT BEING TERMINATED,
A PARTY MAY ASK THE PERSON OR ORGANISATION
STATED IN THE CONTRACT DATA TO CHOOSE A
REPLACEMENT ADJUDICATOR AND THE PARTIES
ACCEPT HIS CHOICE

NEW ADJUDICATOR
CHOSEN

92.2
THE CHOSEN ADJUDICATOR
- IS APPOINTED UNDER THE NEC ADJUDICATOR'S
CONTRACT AND
- BECOMES THE ADJUDICATOR

REPLACEMENT ADJUDICATOR'S
APPOINTMENT

92.2
IS THERE AN
OUTSTANDING
DISPUTE

Yes

No

92.2
IF A DISPUTE HAD BEEN SUBMITTED TO THE
PREVIOUS ADJUDICATOR BUT A DECISION
HAS NOT BEEN GIVEN
- THE REPLACEMENT ADJUDICATOR GIVES
HIS DECISION ON THE DISPUTE AND
- THE DATE OF SUBMISSION OF THE DISPUTE
TO HIM AS ADJUDICATOR IS TAKEN AS THE
DATE OF HIS APPOINTMENT

DATE OF APPOINTMENT

FINISH

Flow chart 92
The *Adjudicator*

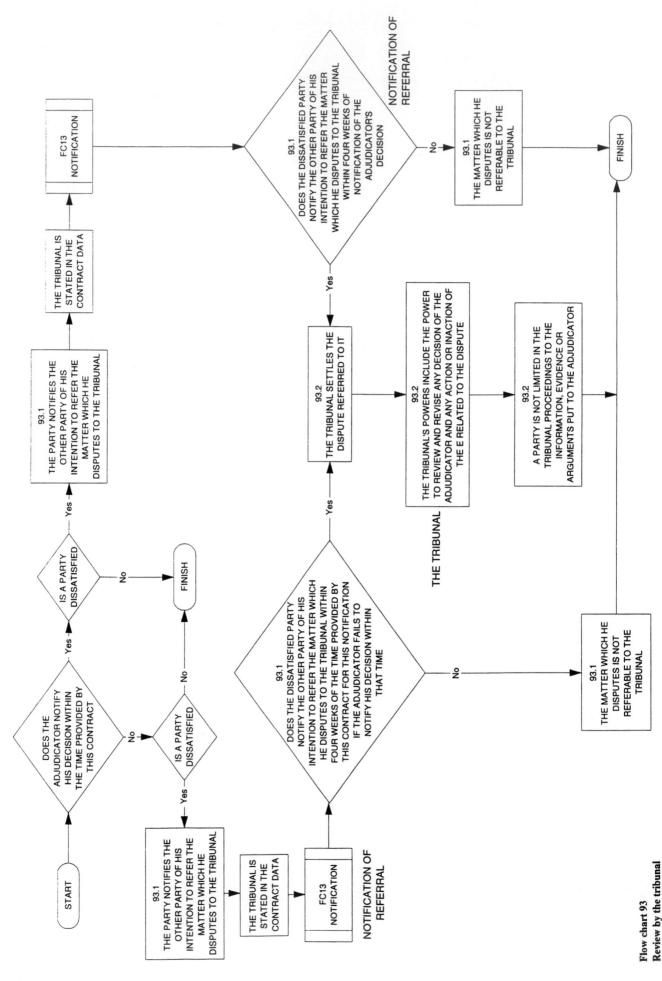

Flow chart 93
Review by the tribunal

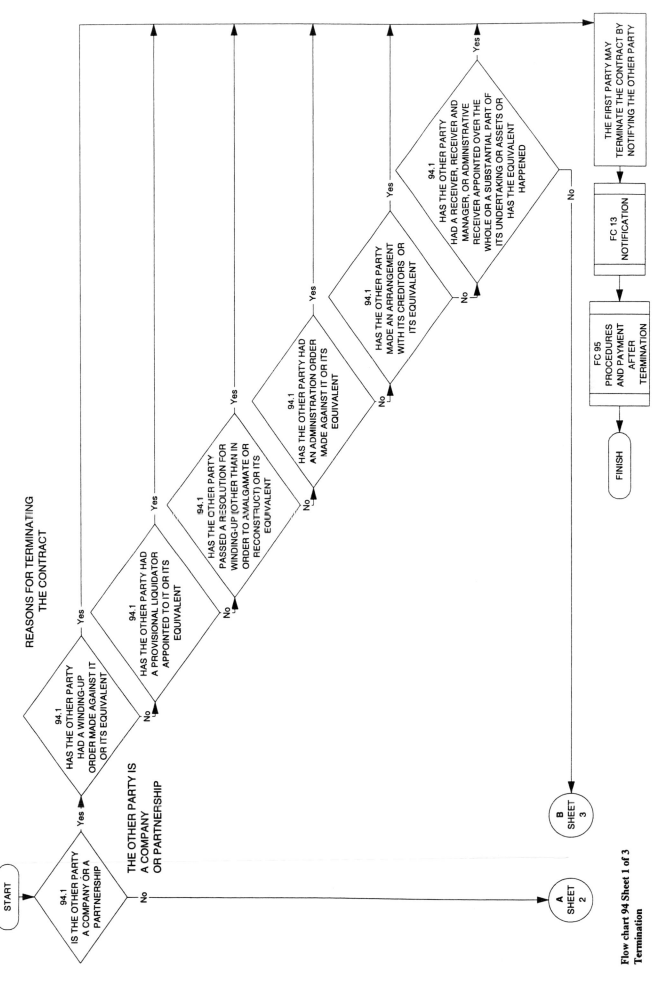

REASONS FOR TERMINATING THE CONTRACT

START

94.1 IS THE OTHER PARTY A COMPANY OR A PARTNERSHIP — No → **A SHEET 2**

THE OTHER PARTY IS A COMPANY OR PARTNERSHIP

Yes

94.1 HAS THE OTHER PARTY HAD A WINDING-UP ORDER MADE AGAINST IT OR ITS EQUIVALENT — Yes

No

94.1 HAS THE OTHER PARTY HAD A PROVISIONAL LIQUIDATOR APPOINTED TO IT OR ITS EQUIVALENT — Yes

No

94.1 HAS THE OTHER PARTY PASSED A RESOLUTION FOR WINDING-UP (OTHER THAN IN ORDER TO AMALGAMATE OR RECONSTRUCT) OR ITS EQUIVALENT — Yes

No

94.1 HAS THE OTHER PARTY HAD AN ADMINISTRATION ORDER MADE AGAINST IT OR ITS EQUIVALENT — Yes

No

94.1 HAS THE OTHER PARTY MADE AN ARRANGEMENT WITH ITS CREDITORS OR ITS EQUIVALENT — Yes

No

94.1 HAS THE OTHER PARTY HAD A RECEIVER, RECEIVER AND MANAGER, OR ADMINISTRATIVE RECEIVER APPOINTED OVER THE WHOLE OR A SUBSTANTIAL PART OF ITS UNDERTAKING OR ASSETS OR HAS THE EQUIVALENT HAPPENED — Yes

No → **B SHEET 3**

THE FIRST PARTY MAY TERMINATE THE CONTRACT BY NOTIFYING THE OTHER PARTY

FC 13 NOTIFICATION

FC 95 PROCEDURES AND PAYMENT AFTER TERMINATION

FINISH

Flow chart 94 Sheet 1 of 3 Termination

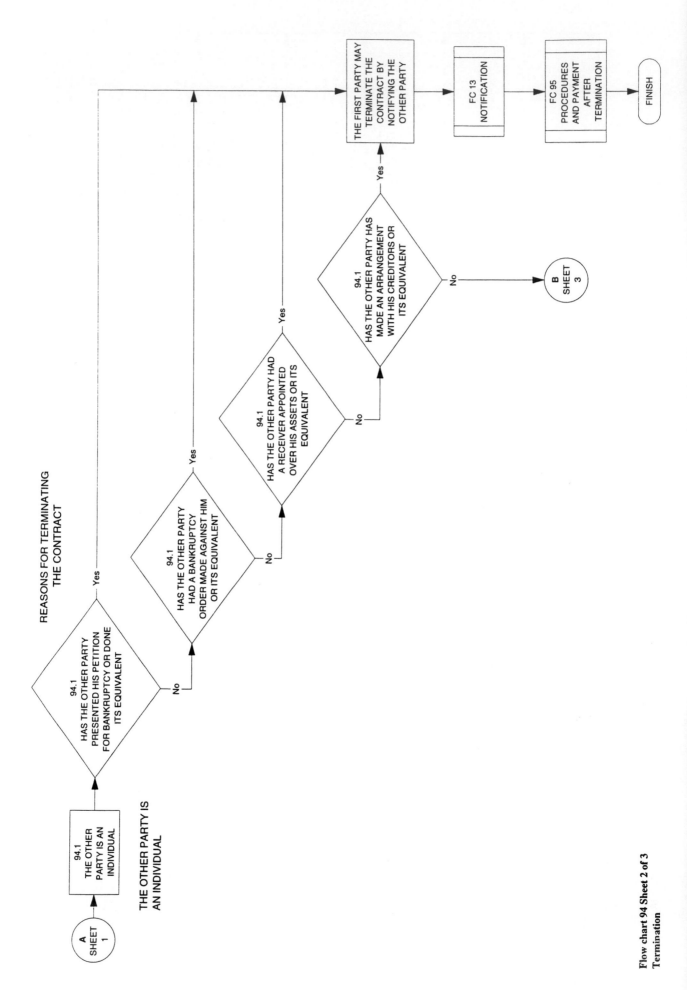

REASONS FOR TERMINATING
THE CONTRACT

THE OTHER PARTY IS
AN INDIVIDUAL

Flow chart 94 Sheet 2 of 3
Termination

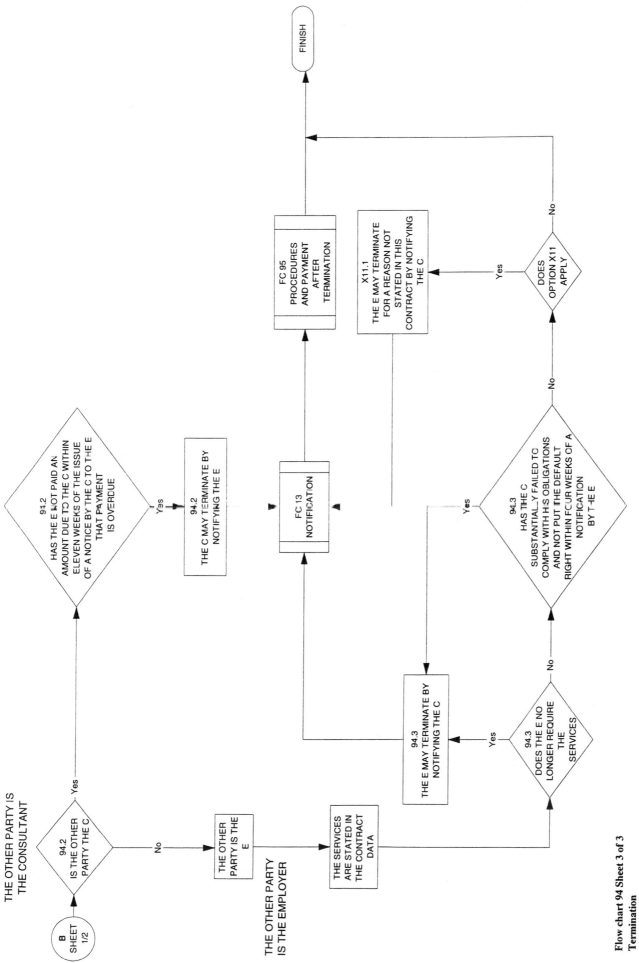

THE OTHER PARTY IS
THE CONSULTANT

B
SHEET
1/2

94.2
IS THE OTHER
PARTY THE C

94.2
HAS THE E NOT PAID AN
AMOUNT DUE TO THE C WITHIN
ELEVEN WEEKS OF THE ISSUE
OF A NOTICE BY THE C TO THE E
THAT PAYMENT
IS OVERDUE

94.2
THE C MAY TERMINATE BY
NOTIFYING THE E

FC 13
NOTIFICATION

FC 95
PROCEDURES
AND PAYMENT
AFTER
TERMINATION

FINISH

X11.1
THE E MAY TERMINATE
FOR A REASON NOT
STATED IN THIS
CONTRACT BY NOTIFYING
THE C

DOES
OPTION X11
APPLY

94.3
HAS THE C
SUBSTANTIALLY FAILED TO
COMPLY WITH HIS OBLIGATIONS
AND NOT PUT THE DEFAULT
RIGHT WITHIN FOUR WEEKS OF A
NOTIFICATION
BY THE E

94.3
THE E MAY TERMINATE BY
NOTIFYING THE C

94.3
DOES THE E NO
LONGER REQUIRE
THE
SERVICES

THE OTHER PARTY
IS THE EMPLOYER

THE OTHER PARTY IS THE
E

THE SERVICES
ARE STATED IN
THE CONTRACT
DATA

**Flow chart 94 Sheet 3 of 3
Termination**

FINAL PAYMENT IN ALL CASES

START

95.1

AFTER TERMINATION
- THE C DOES NO FURTHER WORK NECESSARY TO PROVIDE THE SERVICES
- THE E MAY COMPLETE THE SERVICES HIMSELF OR EMPLOY OTHER PEOPLE TO DO SO, AND MAY USE HIMSELF OR MAKE AVAILABLE TO THOSE OTHER PEOPLE HIS RIGHTS OVER MATERIAL PREPARED BY THE C, OR A SUBCONSULTANT
- THE E MAY REQUIRE THE C TO ASSIGN THE BENEFIT OF ANY SUBCONSULTANCY OR OTHER CONTRACT RELATED TO PERFORMANCE OF THIS CONTRACT TO THE E, AND
- THE PARTIES CONTINUE TO COMPLY WITH THE RESTRICTIONS AND OBLIGATIONS IN THIS CONTRACT ON
    - THE USE OF MATERIAL PREPARED OR OBTAINED BY THE C AND
    - PUBLICISING THE SERVICES

THE SERVICES ARE STATED IN THE CONTRACT DATA

95.1

AFTER THE FINAL PAYMENT HAS BEEN MADE, THE C GIVES TO THE E INFORMATION RESULTING FROM WORK CARRIED OUT TO DATE AND INFORMATION THE C HAS OBTAINED WHICH HE HAS A RESPONSIBILITY TO PROVIDE UNDER THIS CONTRACT

95.2

A FINAL PAYMENT IS MADE AS SOON AS POSSIBLE AFTER TERMINATION. THE AMOUNT DUE ON TERMINATION INCLUDES
- AN AMOUNT DUE ASSESSED AS FOR NORMAL PAYMENTS
- OTHER COSTS REASONABLY INCURRED BY THE C IN EXPECTATION OF COMPLETING THE WHOLE OF THE SERVICES AND TO WHICH THE C IS COMMITTED AND
- ANY AMOUNTS RETAINED BY THE E

INSOLVENCY OF THE CONSULTANT

95.3

HAS THE E TERMINATED BECAUSE OF THE INSOLVENCY OF THE C

No → / Yes →

95.3

THE AMOUNT DUE ON TERMINATION INCLUDES A DEDUCTION OF THE FORECAST OF THE ADDITIONAL COST TO THE E OF COMPLETING THE SERVICES

FAILURE TO PERFORM

95.3

HAS THE E TERMINATED BECAUSE OF THE SUBSTANTIAL FAILURE OF THE C TO COMPLY WITH HIS OBLIGATIONS

No / Yes

X11.1

THE E MAY TERMINATE FOR A REASON NOT STATED IN THIS CONTRACT BY NOTIFYING THE C

X11.2

DOES THE E TERMINATE FOR A REASON NOT STATED IN THIS CONTRACT

Yes / No

FC13
NOTIFICATION

X11.2

AN ADDITIONAL AMOUNT IS DUE ON TERMINATION WHICH IS 5% OF THE DIFFERENCE BETWEEN
- THE FORECAST OF THE FINAL TOTAL OF THE PRICES IN THE ABSENCE OF TERMINATION AND
- THE TOTAL OF THE OTHER AMOUNTS AND COSTS INCLUDED IN THE AMOUNT OTHERWISE DUE ON TERMINATION

DOES OPTION X11 APPLY

Yes / No

A SHEET 2

Flow chart 95 Sheet 1 of 2
Procedures and payment after termination

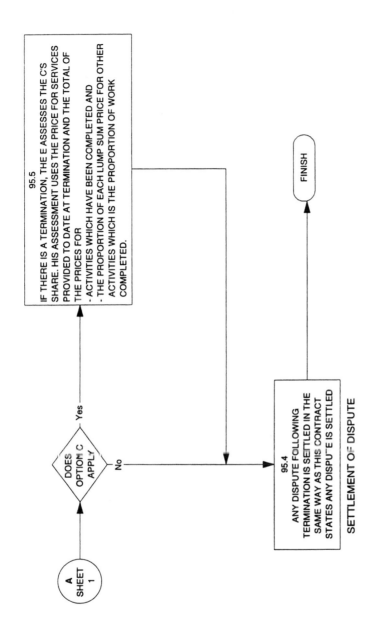

95.5

IF THERE IS A TERMINATION, THE E ASSESSES THE C'S SHARE. HIS ASSESSMENT USES THE PRICE FOR SERVICES PROVIDED TO DATE AT TERMINATION AND THE TOTAL OF THE PRICES FOR
- ACTIVITIES WHICH HAVE BEEN COMPLETED AND
- THE PROPORTION OF EACH LUMP SUM PRICE FOR OTHER ACTIVITIES WHICH IS THE PROPORTION OF WORK COMPLETED.

DOES OPTION C APPLY

Yes

No

FINISH

95.4

ANY DISPUTE FOLLOWING TERMINATION IS SETTLED IN THE SAME WAY AS THIS CONTRACT STATES ANY DISPUTE IS SETTLED

SETTLEMENT OF DISPUTE

A SHEET 1

Flow chart 95 Sheet 2 of 2
Procedures and payment after termination

109

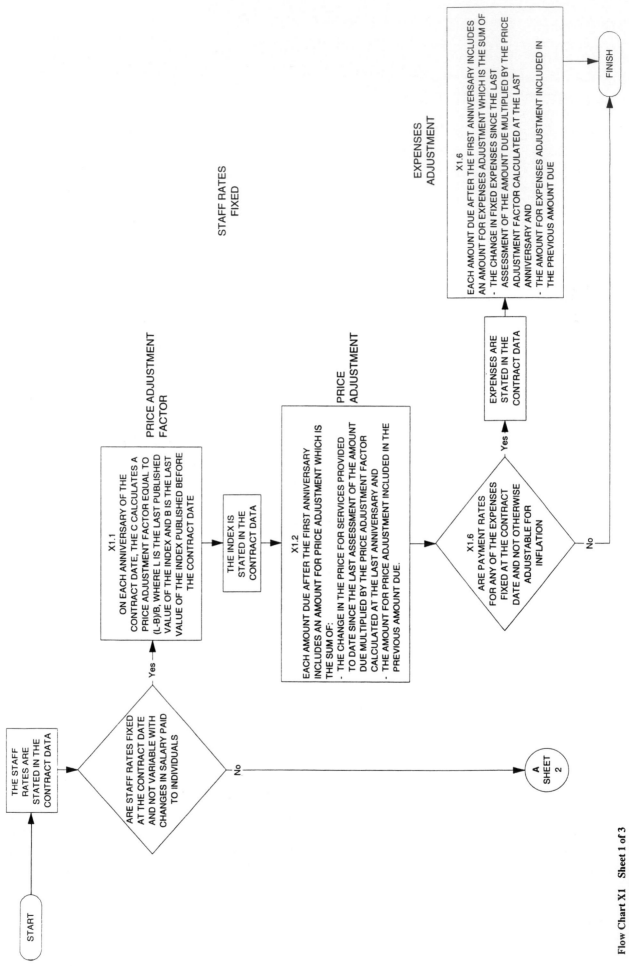

STAFF RATES
FIXED

PRICE ADJUSTMENT
FACTOR

X1.1

ON EACH ANNIVERSARY OF THE
CONTRACT DATE, THE C CALCULATES A
PRICE ADJUSTMENT FACTOR EQUAL TO
(L-B)/B, WHERE L IS THE LAST PUBLISHED
VALUE OF THE INDEX AND B IS THE LAST
VALUE OF THE INDEX PUBLISHED BEFORE
THE CONTRACT DATE

THE INDEX IS
STATED IN THE
CONTRACT DATA

PRICE
ADJUSTMENT

X1.2

EACH AMOUNT DUE AFTER THE FIRST ANNIVERSARY
INCLUDES AN AMOUNT FOR PRICE ADJUSTMENT WHICH IS
THE SUM OF:
- THE CHANGE IN THE PRICE FOR SERVICES PROVIDED
  TO DATE SINCE THE LAST ASSESSMENT OF THE AMOUNT
  DUE MULTIPLIED BY THE PRICE ADJUSTMENT FACTOR
  CALCULATED AT THE LAST ANNIVERSARY AND
- THE AMOUNT FOR PRICE ADJUSTMENT INCLUDED IN THE
  PREVIOUS AMOUNT DUE.

EXPENSES
ADJUSTMENT

X1.6

EACH AMOUNT DUE AFTER THE FIRST ANNIVERSARY INCLUDES
AN AMOUNT FOR EXPENSES ADJUSTMENT WHICH IS THE SUM OF
- THE CHANGE IN FIXED EXPENSES SINCE THE LAST
  ASSESSMENT OF THE AMOUNT DUE MULTIPLIED BY THE PRICE
  ADJUSTMENT FACTOR CALCULATED AT THE LAST
  ANNIVERSARY AND
- THE AMOUNT FOR EXPENSES ADJUSTMENT INCLUDED IN
  THE PREVIOUS AMOUNT DUE

EXPENSES ARE
STATED IN THE
CONTRACT DATA

X1.6

ARE PAYMENT RATES
FOR ANY OF THE EXPENSES
FIXED AT THE CONTRACT
DATE AND NOT OTHERWISE
ADJUSTABLE FOR
INFLATION

THE STAFF
RATES ARE
STATED IN THE
CONTRACT DATA

ARE STAFF RATES FIXED
AT THE CONTRACT DATE
AND NOT VARIABLE WITH
CHANGES IN SALARY PAID
TO INDIVIDUALS

Yes

No

Yes

No

START

FINISH

A
SHEET
2

Flow Chart X1   Sheet 1 of 3
Price Adjustment For Inflation

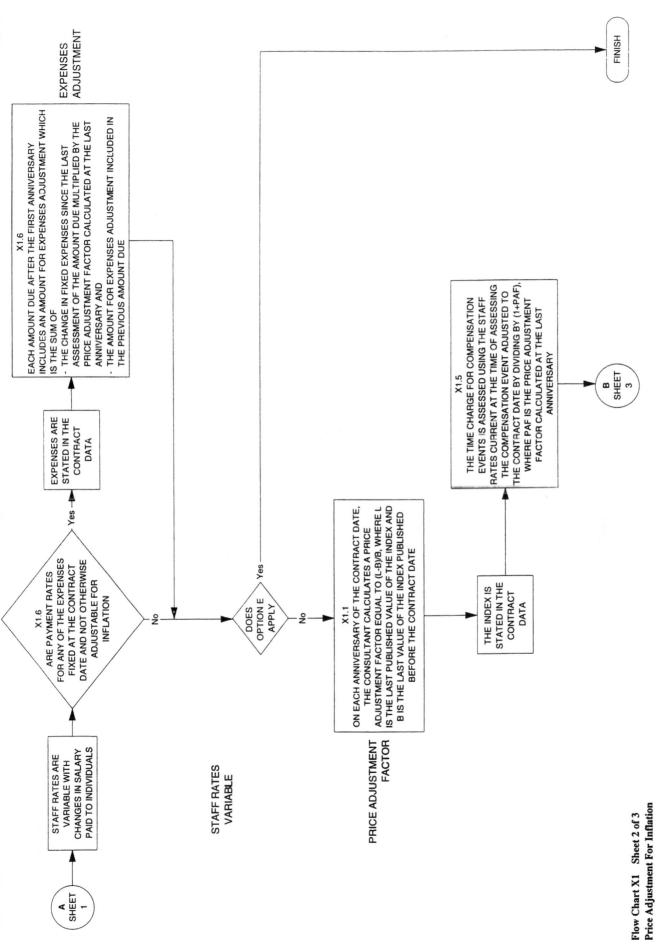

EXPENSES
ADJUSTMENT

X1.6

EACH AMOUNT DUE AFTER THE FIRST ANNIVERSARY
INCLUDES AN AMOUNT FOR EXPENSES ADJUSTMENT WHICH
IS THE SUM OF
- THE CHANGE IN FIXED EXPENSES SINCE THE LAST
  ASSESSMENT OF THE AMOUNT DUE MULTIPLIED BY THE
  PRICE ADJUSTMENT FACTOR CALCULATED AT THE LAST
  ANNIVERSARY AND
- THE AMOUNT FOR EXPENSES ADJUSTMENT INCLUDED IN
  THE PREVIOUS AMOUNT DUE

EXPENSES ARE
STATED IN THE
CONTRACT
DATA

Yes

X1.6

ARE PAYMENT RATES
FOR ANY OF THE EXPENSES
FIXED AT THE CONTRACT
DATE AND NOT OTHERWISE
ADJUSTABLE FOR
INFLATION

No

STAFF RATES ARE
VARIABLE WITH
CHANGES IN SALARY
PAID TO INDIVIDUALS

A
SHEET
1

STAFF RATES
VARIABLE

DOES
OPTION E
APPLY

Yes

No

X1.1

ON EACH ANNIVERSARY OF THE CONTRACT DATE,
THE CONSULTANT CALCULATES A PRICE
ADJUSTMENT FACTOR EQUAL TO (L-B)/B, WHERE L
IS THE LAST PUBLISHED VALUE OF THE INDEX AND
B IS THE LAST VALUE OF THE INDEX PUBLISHED
BEFORE THE CONTRACT DATE

PRICE ADJUSTMENT
FACTOR

THE INDEX IS
STATED IN THE
CONTRACT
DATA

X1.5

THE TIME CHARGE FOR COMPENSATION
EVENTS IS ASSESSED USING THE STAFF
RATES CURRENT AT THE TIME OF ASSESSING
THE COMPENSATION EVENT ADJUSTED TO
THE CONTRACT DATE BY DIVIDING BY (1+PAF),
WHERE PAF IS THE PRICE ADJUSTMENT
FACTOR CALCULATED AT THE LAST
ANNIVERSARY

B
SHEET
3

FINISH

Flow Chart X1   Sheet 2 of 3
Price Adjustment For Inflation

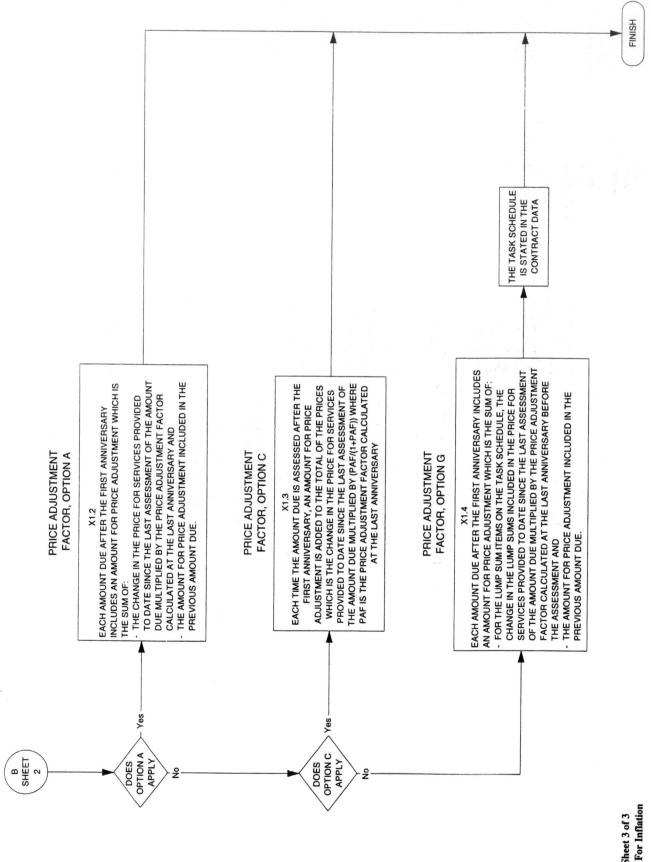

PRICE ADJUSTMENT FACTOR, OPTION A

X1.2

EACH AMOUNT DUE AFTER THE FIRST ANNIVERSARY INCLUDES AN AMOUNT FOR PRICE ADJUSTMENT WHICH IS THE SUM OF:
- THE CHANGE IN THE PRICE FOR SERVICES PROVIDED TO DATE SINCE THE LAST ASSESSMENT OF THE AMOUNT DUE MULTIPLIED BY THE PRICE ADJUSTMENT FACTOR CALCULATED AT THE LAST ANNIVERSARY AND
- THE AMOUNT FOR PRICE ADJUSTMENT INCLUDED IN THE PREVIOUS AMOUNT DUE.

PRICE ADJUSTMENT FACTOR, OPTION C

X1.3

EACH TIME THE AMOUNT DUE IS ASSESSED AFTER THE FIRST ANNIVERSARY, AN AMOUNT FOR PRICE ADJUSTMENT IS ADDED TO THE TOTAL OF THE PRICES WHICH IS THE CHANGE IN THE PRICE FOR SERVICES PROVIDED TO DATE SINCE THE LAST ASSESSMENT OF THE AMOUNT DUE MULTIPLIED BY (PAF/(1+PAF)) WHERE PAF IS THE PRICE ADJUSTMENT FACTOR CALCULATED AT THE LAST ANNIVERSARY

PRICE ADJUSTMENT FACTOR, OPTION G

X1.4

EACH AMOUNT DUE AFTER THE FIRST ANNIVERSARY INCLUDES AN AMOUNT FOR PRICE ADJUSTMENT WHICH IS THE SUM OF:
- FOR THE LUMP SUM ITEMS ON THE TASK SCHEDULE, THE CHANGE IN THE LUMP SUMS INCLUDED IN THE PRICE FOR SERVICES PROVIDED TO DATE SINCE THE LAST ASSESSMENT OF THE AMOUNT DUE MULTIPLIED BY THE PRICE ADJUSTMENT FACTOR CALCULATED AT THE LAST ANNIVERSARY BEFORE THE ASSESSMENT AND
- THE AMOUNT FOR PRICE ADJUSTMENT INCLUDED IN THE PREVIOUS AMOUNT DUE.

THE TASK SCHEDULE IS STATED IN THE CONTRACT DATA

B SHEET 2

DOES OPTION A APPLY — Yes

No

DOES OPTION C APPLY — Yes

No

FINISH

Flow Chart X1   Sheet 3 of 3
Price Adjustment For Inflation

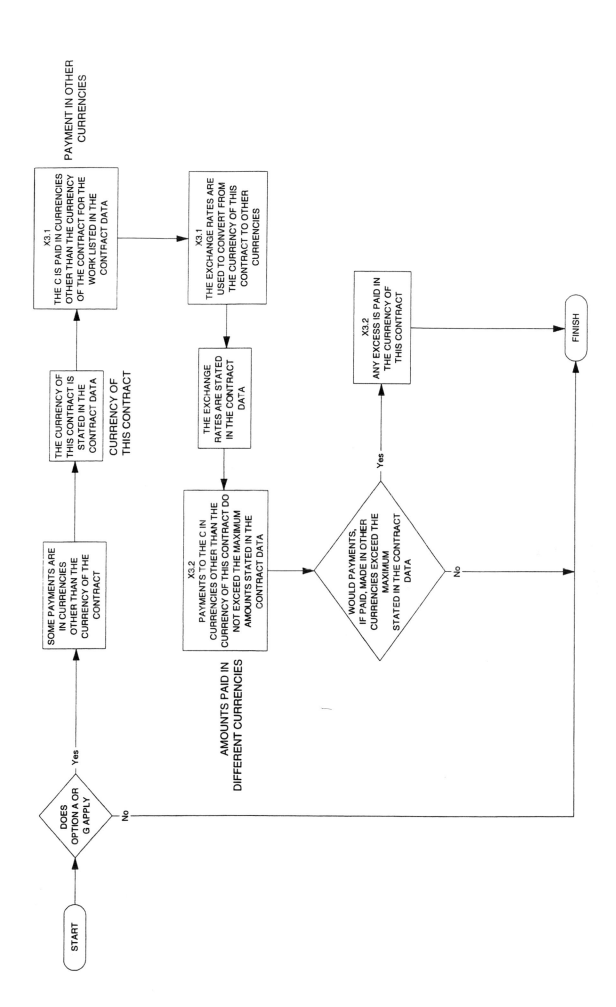

PAYMENT IN OTHER CURRENCIES

X3.1
THE C IS PAID IN CURRENCIES OTHER THAN THE CURRENCY OF THE CONTRACT FOR THE WORK LISTED IN THE CONTRACT DATA

THE CURRENCY OF THIS CONTRACT IS STATED IN THE CONTRACT DATA

CURRENCY OF THIS CONTRACT

SOME PAYMENTS ARE IN CURRENCIES OTHER THAN THE CURRENCY OF THE CONTRACT

START

DOES OPTION A OR G APPLY

Yes

No

X3.1
THE EXCHANGE RATES ARE USED TO CONVERT FROM THE CURRENCY OF THIS CONTRACT TO OTHER CURRENCIES

THE EXCHANGE RATES ARE STATED IN THE CONTRACT DATA

X3.2
PAYMENTS TO THE C IN CURRENCIES OTHER THAN THE CURRENCY OF THIS CONTRACT DO NOT EXCEED THE MAXIMUM AMOUNTS STATED IN THE CONTRACT DATA

AMOUNTS PAID IN DIFFERENT CURRENCIES

WOULD PAYMENTS, IF PAID, MADE IN OTHER CURRENCIES EXCEED THE MAXIMUM STATED IN THE CONTRACT DATA

Yes

No

X3.2
ANY EXCESS IS PAID IN THE CURRENCY OF THIS CONTRACT

FINISH

Flow chart X3
Multiple currencies (used only with options A and G)

113

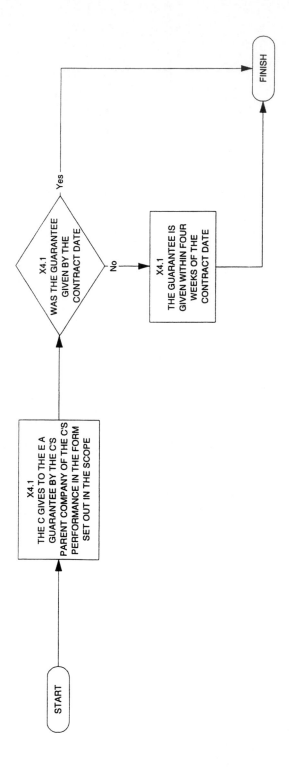

Flow Chart X4
Parent company guarantee

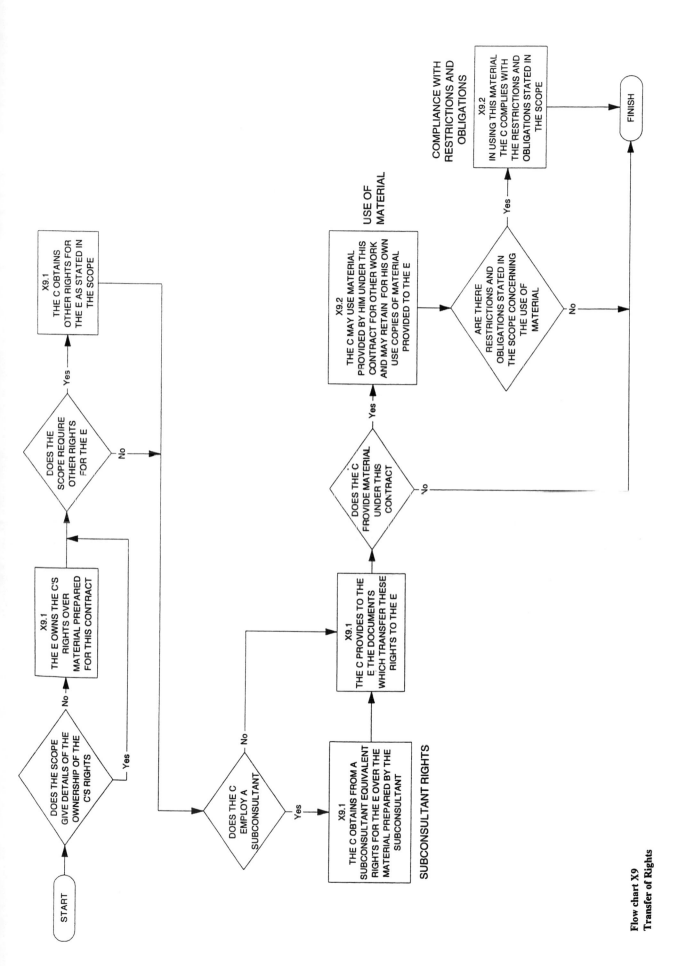

START

DOES THE SCOPE GIVE DETAILS OF THE OWNERSHIP OF THE C'S RIGHTS

No

Yes

X9.1
THE E OWNS THE C'S RIGHTS OVER MATERIAL PREPARED FOR THIS CONTRACT

DOES THE SCOPE REQUIRE OTHER RIGHTS FOR THE E

Yes

No

X9.1
THE C OBTAINS OTHER RIGHTS FOR THE E AS STATED IN THE SCOPE

DOES THE C EMPLOY A SUBCONSULTANT

No

Yes

X9.1
THE C OBTAINS FROM A SUBCONSULTANT EQUIVALENT RIGHTS FOR THE E OVER THE MATERIAL PREPARED BY THE SUBCONSULTANT

SUBCONSULTANT RIGHTS

X9.1
THE C PROVIDES TO THE E THE DOCUMENTS WHICH TRANSFER THESE RIGHTS TO THE E

DOES THE C PROVIDE MATERIAL UNDER THIS CONTRACT

Yes

No

X9.2
THE C MAY USE MATERIAL PROVIDED BY HIM UNDER THIS CONTRACT FOR OTHER WORK AND MAY RETAIN FOR HIS OWN USE COPIES OF MATERIAL PROVIDED TO THE E

USE OF MATERIAL

ARE THERE RESTRICTIONS AND OBLIGATIONS STATED IN THE SCOPE CONCERNING THE USE OF MATERIAL

Yes

No

X9.2
IN USING THIS MATERIAL THE C COMPLIES WITH THE RESTRICTIONS AND OBLIGATIONS STATED IN THE SCOPE

COMPLIANCE WITH RESTRICTIONS AND OBLIGATIONS

FINISH

Flow chart X9
Transfer of Rights

Appendices

APPENDIX 1

SAMPLE FORM OF AGREEMENT

This agreement is made on the ………..…….…….. day of …………………..……….. 19……..……..

between   •   ………………………………………………………………………………(name)

                 of ……………………………………………………..……………………………….

                 (company/organisation) (the Employer)

and   •   ………………………………………………………………..…………….(name)

                 of ……………………………………………………..………………………..………

                 (company/organisation) (the Consultant)

The Employer will pay the Consultant the amount due and carry out his duties in accordance with the conditions of contract identified in the Contract Data.

The Consultant will Provide the Services in accordance with the conditions of contract identified in the Contract Data.

Signed by …………………………………………………………..……………………..

Name ………………………………………………………………………………..

Position …………………………………………………………………………………..

on behalf of (Employer) …………………………………………………………………

and …………………………………………………………………………………………

Name ………………………………………………………………………………………..

Position ……………………………………………………………………………………..

on behalf of (Consultant) …………………………………………..………………………..

ALTERNATIVE IF AGREEMENT IS EXECUTED AS A DEED UNDER ENGLISH LAW

When the Employer is an individual:

- Executed as a deed by

  …………………………………….. (signed)   Signature of Witness ………………………..

  ……………………………………. (Employer) Name of Witness ………………………….

When the Employer is a company:

- Executed as a deed by

  …………………………………….. (signed)

  …………………………………….. (name of Director)

  …………………………………….. (signed)

  …………………………………….. (name of Director or Company Secretary)

When the Consultant is an individual or partnership:

+ Executed as a deed by

Name of individual or partner	Signature	Name of Witness	Signature
…………………………….	…………………………….	…………………………..	………………………….
…………………………….	…………………………….	…………………………..	………………………….
…………………………….	…………………………….	…………………………..	………………………….
…………………………….	…………………………….	…………………………..	………………………….

(Note: All partners to sign except where one is authorised as signatory by deed)

When the Consultant is a Company

+ Executed as a deed by

  …………………………………….. (signed)

  …………………………………….. (name of Director)

  …………………………………….. (Signed)

  …………………………………….. (name of Director or Company Secretary)

- Delete one of these
+ Delete one of these

APPENDIX 2

CONTRACT DATA - worked example

Introduction

The following example shows how the Contract Data should be completed for a contract with a particular selection of decisions made by the *Employer*. It follows that not all the possible optional statements are included in the example. The guidance notes included under "Basis of the appointment of a Consultant" are expanded by illustration.

The Contract Data for a particular contract must be prepared specifically for that contract. When re-typing or otherwise preparing the basic format, it is most important that the text printed in the PSC is not changed because it has been designed to read correctly with the relevant clauses in the PSC. The correct text for each statement is identified in the example by the font in this main text.

Contracts for the provision of professional services by a consultant are sometimes prepared as the outcome of negotiation during which the potential *Consultant* is already advising the *Employer* on the proposed contract between them. It is nevertheless important to recognise the three basic stages of this process which become clearly separate when an employer is seeking bids in competition from several consultants. With respect to the preparation of the Contract Data for a contract under the PSC, these three stages are:

a) *Employer* prepares an enquiry comprising a completed Part one and a prepared format for Part two;

b) bidding consultants prepare their offers by completing Part two;

c) a contract is made between the *Employer* and the successful *Consultant*.

The example assumes that this process is followed and the entries made at each stage are identified by the following fonts:

a) ***European Grain plc***

b) **PM Services Ltd**

c) *Ms. 1. Arkwright*

The example also assumes that the following decisions have been made by the *Employer*:

- main option A has been chosen together with secondary options X1, X2, X3, X4, X8, X9, X10, X11, Y(UK)1, Y(UK)2 & Z;

- the *completion date* for the whole of the *services*;

- a programme is not to be identified in the Contract Data;

- the period for payment of accounts is three weeks (as clause 51.1);

- the amount to be paid for certain *expenses* and the *Consultant* to quote for others;

- the *Consultant* is to provide additional insurances;

- the *Consultant*'s liability is not limited to the amount of his insurances;

- the *tribunal* is arbitration.

It is recommended that, when an optional statement is used in a Contract Data Part one, it is inserted under the appropriate section of the PSC, as illustrated in the example.

Part one - Data provided by the *Employer*

1. General

- The *conditions of contract* are the core clauses and the clauses for Options. **A, X1, X2, X3, X4, X8, X9, X10, X11, Y(UK)1, Y(UK)2, Z.** . . .of the second edition (June 1998) of the NEC Professional Services Contract.

> Choose a main option and the secondary options appropriate to the contract which must be compatible with the chosen main option. See GN on "Contract Strategy" and "Basis of the appointment of a *Consultant*"

> The *Employer*'s legal name

- The *Employer* is

Name. . . . . . **European Grain plc** . . . .

Address . . **Long Acre Industrial Estate** . . . .
. . . . **Spearshead, Bristol BS8 2LR** . . . .
. . . . **Tel 01234 567890 Fax 01234 678905** . . .

> *Employer*'s postal address (Cl. 13.2) including post code, telephone and facsimile numbers for the purpose of the contract (not necessarily the registered address).

> Leave blank until the Parties have jointly agreed an appointee. At Contract Date, state the *Adjudicator*'s name, postal address with post code, telephone and facsimile numbers for the purpose of the contract. See GN on Cl 90.1

- The *Adjudicator* is

Name. . . . *Ms. I. Arkwright* . . . .

Address . . . . *Solva and Smith Project Management* . . . .
. . . . *Meadow House, Goode Road* . . . .
. . . . *Exeter EX8 6LN* . . . .
. . . . *tel 01567 23456* . . . *fax 01567 78901* . .

> Describe the *services* briefly for their general identification.

- The *services* are
. . . **Project management of extensions to unloading** .
. . . **and distribution facilities at Long Acre Works** . . . .

> State references of the documents containing the Scope. See GN on "Basis of the appointment of a Consultant" and Table 2.

- The Scope is in
. . . . . **Document ref XX90**. . . . .

> Clause 12.2

- The *law of the contract* is the law of **England and Wales**

> Clause 13.1

- The *language of this contract* is. . . . . **English** . . . .

- The *period for reply* to a communication is. . . **2** . . . weeks

> GN on Clause 13.3

- The *period for retention* of documents is . . . . **2** . . . . years following Completion or earlier termination.

> GN on Clause 13.5

- The *health and safety requirements* are
. . . . **European Grain Safety Rules** . . . .

> GN on Clause 17.1

- The *additional conditions* of *contract* are:. . . .**Clauses Z1 to Z6 as in document Grain Additional GA 20 dated September 1995** . . . .

> If Option Z is used, refer to GN on Option Z and state the conditions here with reference numbers using prefix "Z".

2. The Parties' main
    responsibilities

- The *Employer* provides access to the following people, places and things

Access to	*access date*
Long acre works and Employer's Agent	**5 January 1998**

- The *Employer's Agent* is

Name . . . . . . **Mr. E.X.E. Cutive.** . . . .
Address. . . . . **Long Acre Industrial Estate** . . . .
. . . . **Spearshead, Bristol BS8 2LR** . . . .

- The authority of the *Employer's Agent* is
. . . . . **all actions by the Employer stated in this contract** . . . .

- The *collateral warranty agreements* are

Agreement Reference	Third Party
. . . . . **NXT/Door-1**	**Adjacent Properties plc**

3. Time

- The *starting date* is . . . . **5 January 1998** . . . .

- The *Consultant* is to submit a first programme for acceptance within . . .**3** . . weeks of the Contract Date.

- The *completion date* for the whole of the *services* is . . . . **31 December 1999** . . . . .

4. Quality

- The quality policy statement and quality plan are provided within . . **3** . . weeks of the Contract Date

- The *defects date* is . . .**26** . . . . . . weeks after Completion of the whole of the *services*.

5. Payment

- The *assessment interval* is . . .**a calendar month** . . . . . .

- The *currency of this contract* is . .**pounds sterling (£)** . .

- The *interest rate* is . . .**2** . . .% per annum above . . . **base lending rate of Lloyds Bank plc** . . . .

- The *expenses* stated by the *Employer* are

Item	Amount
. . . . **car mileage**	**35 p per mile** . . . .
. . . . **rail travel**	**standard class fare** . . . . . .

- The *Consultant* prepares forecasts of the total *expenses* for the *services* at intervals no longer than . . . . .**12** . . . . .weeks

Side notes (boxes):

GN on clause 26.1

If Option X10 is used, See GN on Option X10

If Option X8 is used, the details of any *collateral warranty agreements* should be referred to here and appended to the Contract Data. See GN on Option X8.

GN on clause 31.2

If no programme is to be identified in Part two of the Contract Data. See GN on Clause 31.1.

If the Employer decides *completion date*. GN on clause 30.1

Clause 40.2

GN on clause 41.1

Can be any period but preferably not longer than 5 weeks. See GN on Cl 50.1

Clause 51.2

GN on Clause 51.5

If the *Employer* states any *expenses* and the amount to be paid. See GN on Clause 50.3

GN on clause 52

- Payment for work listed below will be made in the currencies stated

Work	Currency	Maximum amount

Consultancy on design . . . . . . **DM** . . . . **DM** . . **30,000** . . .
of loading equipment . . . .

If Option X3 is used. See GN on Option X3.

- The *exchange rates* are those published in . . . .
. . . .***Financial Times*** . . . . .on. . . .***1 December 1997*** . . . .

- The *index* is . . . . . **the Retail Price Index** . . . .

If Option X1 is used. See GN on Option X1.

6. Compensation events
- The *applicable law* is . . **Law of England and Wales**. . .
. . . **German Law**. . . . . . .

If Option X2 is used. See GN on Option X2.

8. Indemnity insurance and liability
- The amounts of insurance and the periods for which the *Consultant* maintains insurance are

Event	Cover	Period following Completion of the whole of the *services* or earlier termination
failure of the *Consultant* to use the skill and care normally used by professionals providing services similar to the *services*.	. . . . **£5m** . . . . . in respect of each claim, without limit to the number of claims.	. . **6 years**. . . ..
bodily injury to or death of a person (not an employee of the *Consultant*) or loss of or damage to property resulting from an action or failure to take action by the *Consultant*.	. . . . **£5m** . . . . . in respect of each claim, without limit to the number of claims.	**12 months**
bodily injury to or death of employees of the *Consultant* arising out of and in course of their employment in connection with this contract	. . . . **£2m** . . . . . in respect of each claim, without limit to the number of claims.	**12 months**

GN on Clause 81.1

- The *Employer* provides the following insurances

| **Liability for loss of or damage to property (except survey equipment) provided by the Employer for the use of the Consultant.** | **The replacement cost until the property is returned to the Employer.** |

GN on Clause 82.1

- The *Consultant*'s liability to the *Employer* resulting from a failure to Provide the Services is limited to

... **the amount of the Consultant** *'s insurance cover.* . . . .

- The *Consultant* provides these additional insurances

If the *Consultant* is to provide additional insurances see GN on Clause 81.1.

1. Insurance against . . **liability for loss of or damage to survey equipment provided by the Employer.**
   Cover is . . . . **replacement cost.** . . . .
   Period of Cover . . **until all the equipment is returned to the Employer** . . . .
   Deductibles are. . . . . **nil.** . . . .

9. Disputes and termination

State the appropriate professional organisation see Clause 92.2

- The person or organisation who will choose a replacement adjudicator if the Parties cannot agree a choice is
  . . . . . . **The Institution of Civil Engineers** . . . .

- The *tribunal* is . . . . **arbitration** . . . .

GN on Clause 93.1

- The arbitration procedure is
  . . . . **The ICE Arbitration Procedure 1997.** . . . .

If the *tribunal* is arbitration state the Arbitration Procedure to be used. See GN on Clause 93.1

Part two - Data provided by the *Consultant*

- The *Consultant* is

Name . . . . . . **PM Services Ltd** . . . .

Address . . . . . **Enterprise Way** . . . .
. . . . **Bristol** . . . .
. . . . **BS90 6PM** . . . .

> Bidding consultant to state legal name and postal address (with post code) for the purpose of the contract.
> See Clause 13.2

> *Employer* to state key jobs. Bidding consultant to name proposed *key persons*.
> See GN on Clause 22.1

- The *key persons* and their jobs are

Job	*Key persons*
. . . . *Project Manager*	.Ms. K. Smithson . . . . . .
. . . . *Estimator*	.Mr. W. Jones . . . .
. . . . *Planner*	.Ms. J. Brown . . . .
. . . . **Chief Designer**	.Mr. V. Green . . . .

- The *staff rates* are

Name/Designation	Rate
Ms. K. Smithson (PM)	£75 per hour
Mr. W. Jones (Estimator)	£60 per hour
Ms. J. Brown (Planner)	£60 per hour
Assistants	£35 per hour

> Bidding consultant to quote *staff rates* for the different categories (or names) of staff.
> See GN on clause 11.2(11).

- The *expenses* stated by the *Consultant* are

> If the *Consultant* states the *expenses* and the amount to be paid. (These can be in addition to those stated by the *Employer* in the Contract Data Part one).
> See GN on Clause 50.3

Item	Amount
Subsistence (as authorised away from home address)	**£80 per night**
Printing of drawings	**£5.50 per A1 size print**

- The *Employer* provides access to the following people, places and things

> GN on clause 26.1

Access to	*access date*
Designers of loading equipment	**12 January 1998**

> If Option A or C is used bidding consultant to state reference of his priced *activity schedule*.
> See GN on *activity schedule*

- The *activity schedule* is . . . .**AS 1** . . . .

APPENDIX 3

ADAPTATION FOR SUBCONTRACTS WHERE A CONTRACTOR IS EMPLOYED UNDER THE ECC AND WISHES TO APPOINT A CONSULTANT UNDER THE PSC

The adapted PSC can be used for a subcontract by a *Contractor* employed under the ECC wishing to appoint a *Consultant* to provide professional services (ECC cl 26.3) e.g. design. In these circumstances the following guidance is given

Additional conditions

The following clauses should be added under the PSC Option Z:

Z1 In these *conditions of contract* and the Contract Data, the following terms are amended as shown

Term in PSC	Term to be used in subcontract
Contract Data	Subcontract Data
Employer	*Contractor*
Consultant	*Subcontractor*
Subconsultant	Subsubcontractor
Contract Date	Subcontract Date
this contract	this subcontract
subcontract	subsubcontract
law of the contract	*law of the subcontract*
language of this contract	*language of this subcontract*
currency of this contract	*currency of this subcontract*

Z2 In these *conditions of contract* the periods of time in the clauses stated are changed as follows:

PSC clause	Time in PSC clause	Time in subcontract clause
51.1	three weeks	four weeks
61.1	two weeks	one week
62.3 first sentence	two weeks	one week
62.3 second sentence	two weeks	four weeks
90.1 top section of the Adjudication table	the second occurrence of four weeks	three weeks
90.1 middle section of the Adjudication table	the second occurrence of four weeks	three weeks
93.1 second sentence	four weeks	three weeks
Option G 55.3 last sentence	two weeks	one week
Option G 55.5 first sentence	four weeks	five weeks
Option Y(UK)2 Y2.3, additional clause 56.1 2nd bullet.	seven days	fourteen days

Other matters to be considered

Scope

The PSC guidance notes are wholly relevant. The *Contractor* should pay particular attention to his preparation of the Scope and ensure that his obligations in the main contract with respect to the subcontracted *services* are properly undertaken by the Subcontractor.

Subcontract Data

The following basic information about the main contract should be included in the Subcontract Data (as in the Engineering and Construction Subcontract):

- title of the *works*
- the *Employer*
- the *Project Manager*
- the *Supervisor*
- the *Adjudicator*

Main option

The main option chosen for the PSC subcontract need not be the same type as the main option in the ECC main contract. For example, a *Contractor* employed on an ECC Option E cost reimbursable contract may require design work to be done on a PSC Option A activity schedule subcontract.

Time periods

As well as the periods of time adjusted in the Option Z additional conditions suggested above, other time periods are to be stated in the Subcontract Data (e.g. the *period for reply*). The *Contractor* must ensure that these periods are adequate for him to be able to comply with the main contract.

Termination

In order to provide for the possibility of the main contract being terminated, the *Contractor* will usually wish to include the PSC Option X11 in the subcontract.

Disputes

Provision for joint adjudication of disputes is made in PSC clause 91.3. The *main contract Adjudicator* should be identified in the Subcontract Data.

Insurance

The *Employer*'s risks remain and the *Contractor* passes those of his risks under the ECC to the *Consultant* (Subcontractor) where they apply to the subcontract *services*. Double insurance is effectively avoided since the insurance premiums payable by the *Contractor* under the main contract (ECC) will reflect the proportion of the services which are subcontracted.

Where the *Consultant* is likely to complete Providing the Services some time before the ECC Completion Date and defects date, careful consideration will need to be given to the periods for which insurance by the *Consultant* is required. Where Option M is not included in the main contract (ECC), the standard of care required of the *Consultant* is a matter of negotiation between the *Contractor* and the *Consultant*. The PSC provides for "the skill and care normally used by professionals providing the services similar to the *services*".

The *Consultant* will be required to provide Employer's Liability Insurance, to cover his own employees, since the latter would not be covered by the *Contractor*'s insurance.

APPENDIX 4

ADAPTATION FOR SUBCONTRACTS WHERE A CONSULTANT IS EMPLOYED UNDER THE PSC AND WISHES TO APPOINT A SUBCONSULTANT UNDER THE PSC

The adapted PSC can be used for a subcontract by a *Consultant* employed under the PSC wishing to appoint a *Subconsultant* to provide part of the *services* (cl 24.3). In these circumstances the following guidance is given.

Additional conditions

The following clauses should be add under the PSC Option Z:

Z1 In these *conditions of contract* and the Contract Data, the following terms are amended as shown

Term in PSC	Term to be used in subcontract
Contract Data	Subcontract Data
Employer	*Consultant*
Consultant	*Subconsultant*
Subconsultant	*Subsubconsultant*
Contract Date	Subcontract Date
this contract	this subcontract
subcontract	subsubcontract
law of the contract	*law of the subcontract*
language of this contract	*language of this subcontract*
currency of this contract	*currency of this subcontract*

Z2 In these *conditions of contract* the periods of time in the clauses stated are changed as follows.

PSC clause	Time in PSC clause	Time in subcontract clause
51.1	three weeks	four weeks
61.1	two weeks	one week
62.3 first sentence	two weeks	one week
62.3 second sentence	two weeks	four weeks
90.1 top section of the Adjudication Table	the second occurrence of four weeks	three weeks
90.1 middle section of the Adjudication table	the second occurrence of four weeks	three weeks
93.1 second sentence	four weeks	three weeks
Option G 55.3 - last sentence	two weeks	one week
Option G 55.5 - first sentence	four weeks	five weeks
Option Y(UK)2 Y2.3, additional clause 56.1 2nd bullet.	seven days	fourteen days

Other matters to be considered

Scope

The PSC guidance notes are wholly relevant.

Subcontract Data

The following basic information about the main contract should be included in the Subcontract Data:

- title of the *services*
- the *Employer*
- the *Adjudicator*

Main option

The main option chosen for the PSC subcontract need not be the same as that chosen for the main contract. For example, a *Consultant* employed on an Option E time based contract may decide to appoint a Subconsultant on an Option A priced subcontract with *activity schedule*.

Time periods

As well as the periods of time adjusted in the Option Z additional conditions suggested above, other time periods are to be stated in the Subcontract Data (e.g. the *period for reply*). The *Consultant* must ensure that these periods are adequate for him to be able to comply with the main contract.

Termination

In order to provide for the possibility of the main contract being terminated, the *Consultant* will usually wish to include the PSC Option X11 in the subcontract.

Disputes

Provision for joint adjudication of disputes is made in PSC clause 91.3. The *main contract Adjudicator* should be identified in the Subcontract Data.

Insurance

The *Employer*'s risks remain and the *Consultant* passes those of his risks under the PSC to the *Subconsultant* where they apply to the subcontract *services*. Double insurance is effectively avoided since the insurance premiums payable by the *Consultant* under the PSC will reflect the proportion of the *services* which are subcontracted to the *Subconsultant*.

Where the *Subconsultant* is likely to complete Providing the Services some time before Completion of the *Consultant*'s services, careful consideration will need to be given to the periods for which insurance by the *Subconsultant* is required.

The *Subconsultant* will be required to provide Employer's Liability Insurance to cover his own employees, since the latter will not be covered by the *Consultant*'s insurance.

NEC PROFESSIONAL SERVICES CONTRACT GUIDANCE NOTES

Index by page numbers, followed (where appropriate) by clause numbers in square brackets [ ] main clause heads are indicated by bold page numbers, option clauses by their letters and flow charts by [FC]. Terms in *italics* are identified in the Contract Data, and defined terms have capital initial letters.

Abbreviations: CDM = Construction (Design and Management) Regulations 1994; HGCR = Housing Grants, Construction and Regeneration Act 1996 (Option Y(UK)2); PSC = Professional Services Contract.